Pl

I consider it an honor t[illegible]ve met you and I give God all the glory for what He has started in your life and for using you. This book is only the beginning George, may you be guided by the Holy Spirit all the days of your life. Love, Mo.

—Mojisola Adeniran Ani, Abouja, Nigeria

To know God and make Him known, this is our mission. To know His Presence and to teach others to do the same, this is our calling. To love Him and be loved by Him, this is our privilege. But to rest in His fullness and the fullness of His Presence, this for us is the ultimate joy! Real joy, peace, love and happiness can only be enjoyed in the fullness of His Manifest Presence. He is the Alpha, the Omega, the beginning and the end and He longs for nothing more than to simply spend time with us, His priesthood, His peculiar people, His children. This book is a frank illustration of the Presence and impact that our God longs to have in our lives. Oh that we would only let Him!

A must read for those seeking a deeper understanding of the Presence of God. Whether you have been saved for fifty years or you are a new born babe in Christ, this book is sure to inspire you to a deeper, more intimate and loving walk with the Holy Spirit and our Lord and Savior Jesus Christ.

In His Presence

—Ramón R. Raveneau Esq., Castries, Saint Lucia

IN HIS MANIFEST PRESENCE

IN HIS MANIFEST PRESENCE

George G. Jhagroo

Tate Publishing & *Enterprises*

Published by Tate Publishing & Enterprises, LLC
127 E. Trade Center Terrace | Mustang, Oklahoma 73064 USA
1.888.361.9473 | www.tatepublishing.com

Tate Publishing is committed to excellence in the publishing industry. The company reflects the philosophy established by the founders, based on Psalm 68:11,
"The Lord gave the word and great was the company of those who published it."

Cover design by Blake Brasor
Interior design by Jeff Fisher
Illustrations by Maria Jhagroo

Published in the United States of America

ISBN: 978-1-61566-246-3
Religion, Spirituality
10.07.21

DEDICATION

To my closest and dearest Friend,
my Precious Holy Ghost.
You are the Love of my life, my Everything.
You are all I have, and all I will ever need.

This is for You.

RELEVANT SCRIPTURE REFERENCES

"He that hath my commandments, and keepeth them, he it is that loveth me: and he that loveth me shall be loved of my Father, and I will love him, and will manifest myself to him" (John 14:21 KJV).

"But the manifestation of the Spirit is given to every man to profit withal" (1 Corinthians 12:7).

"Blessed are the pure in heart: for they shall see God" (Matthew 5:8).

TABLE OF CONTENTS

FOREWORD

Is there more to Christianity than just believing in God and attending Church? Do you want to know more about having a personal relationship with the third Person of the Holy Trinity, the Holy Ghost? Is it possible to fellowship with Him in a personal and more intimate way as never imagined before? Would the Holy Ghost appear to you as He did to those great men of the Bible so long ago such as Moses, Enoch, David, Elijah, and Daniel, or were those events just a thing of the past and not possible in today's world? In this book George G. Jhagroo shares his experiences as a young man in university faced with a terrible illness, which forced him to make a choice—one of the most important choices of his life, one that would totally transform his life forever. As you read, you will discover how he met the Holy Ghost face to face and how he has walked with Him hand in hand ever since that day with an unquenchable desire for more and more of God's secrets.

As his wife, I am constantly exposed to the reality of the Manifest Presence of God walking the hallways of our home. I have been amazed to see my husband stand and converse with an invisible God whose Manifest Presence is only detectable by His awesome and glorious power permeating throughout the house, to such an extent that I could be in the kitchen and know just when He has arrived.

If you would like a face to face encounter and a hand in hand walk with the Holy Ghost, then I urge you to read on, and as you read on, my humble wish is that you too will experience His Manifest Presence.

—Maria Linda Jhagroo

INTRODUCTION

ON THE SUNDAY morning after my baptism, I was awakened by the sound of a voice calling my name saying, "George, George, I love you. George, George, I love you. George, please wake up."

I sat up in bed and replied loudly to the voice that was speaking to me, "Who are you?" Then all of a sudden I saw it. In the right hand corner of my room next to the dresser, was a radiating power that was so beautifully joyous and yet it filled me with awe. I felt like it would burn or consume the very skin off my bones. So I leaped off the side of the bed and hid behind it, using the bed between us for cover. Although I hid behind the bed, the room was filled with a cool thick dense mist like atmosphere of indescribable joy, and a cool wind kept circulating in the room. I was not afraid of it.

I was just amazed at what I was witnessing. I peeped up over the top of my bed and saw it. There was a person standing about seven feet tall with the figure and shape of a man cloaked in a gloriously bright gown, radiating His glorious power and joy everywhere. He was looking right at me and smiling.

I asked Him, "Who or what are you?"

He looked me square in the eyes and replied, "I am the God of Abraham, Isaac, and Jacob, and I will be your God too if you let me." He stood there with all of His glory on, radiating such an abundance of power and overwhelming joy that my jaw dropped in awe. I stood up with my eyes riveted in the direction from which His glory radiated and emanated until His glory filled the room. It was wonderful, like Heaven itself. There was joy everywhere. He began to speak.

HE TOUCHED ME

SUMMER BREAK HAD arrived. It was June 1997, and my mother was on her way to Belfast, Northern Ireland to visit my younger sister, Ranita, who was in hospital there. She had been studying medicine at Queen's University, my mother's *alma mater* and was about to sit her finals when she became ill and was hospitalized, so Mom flew over to be with her and so did I. We did not know the details of my sister's illness at the time because we were still awaiting a diagnosis. However, what was to happen to me there was surprising and unexpected.

My mother rented a two bedroom apartment where we would stay while we were in Belfast, and it was conveniently located a few minutes away from the hospital. I was excited to return to the land of my birth, but wished I was returning under happier circumstances. I had not been back to Belfast since my family left in the heat of "the Troubles" in 1976 when I was only five-years-old and too young to remember the city.

On my third day there, after my mother and I ate lunch, I went to wash my hands in the bathroom and then accompany her to the hospital. While washing my hands, I was suddenly bombarded with thoughts of Ranita's illness, all the reading and assignments I had to catch up with, and the fear of facing exams that were five months away—one negative and sad thought after another. By the time I was drying my hands, I suddenly burst into tears with uncontrollable grief, and I found myself doubled-over the sink crying inconsolably. Agony inside of me which I never knew lurked there, tied my stomach and throat into knots, and I wept to relieve the pain. The more I wept, the sadder I became causing me to weep even more, unable to stop. The bout of sadness lasted for about five minutes, but before it ended, my mother overheard my sobbing and found me crying in the bathroom. I had never experienced anything like this before in my life, so when Mom asked me why I was crying, I told her the truth and said I didn't know. I did not know why I was crying. All I knew was that I was very sad deep down inside, and the sadness overpowered me like a river bursting its banks and was too much to cope with. It was never ending and try as I may, I could not stop crying. I just had to wait until the sad spell was over. For the first time in my life, I was genuinely afraid because there was something wrong with me, and I did not know what it was. All I knew was that from this moment of my life, I no longer had control over my emotions, they had power over me and I would be at their mercy.

My mother held me, puzzled at what was happening to me and asked me how long this was going on. I explained how I was feeling at that moment, about my sadness and that I had been feeling *low* for a few weeks now. The *low* periods were periods of sadness that lasted about five minutes and occurred once or twice a week, but they were never so intense as to cause me to cry. I would just feel sad for a short while, and after it passed, I would be my old cheerful self again.

The next day my mother made arrangements for me to see a psychiatrist friend of hers, an old colleague from Queens University. He was an older orange-haired Irishman with an orange beard (I had never met anyone with orange hair before, let alone one with an orange beard), and he was no more than five feet five inches in height and had the tiniest little feet. He was one of the nicest and most sympathetic men I have ever met. He was very pleasant to me, gentle and very understanding of my plight. He took me into his office to "have a little chat" as he called it, and he asked my mother to return for me in an hour. We talked about everything that was going on in my life at present, and he asked me to describe the symptoms and what the sadness felt like. At the end of the session, he diagnosed my condition as clinical depression, which was in its early stages and which would worsen if it remained untreated. He prescribed a mild anti-depressant to be taken once daily, and I said good-bye and thanked him.

* * *

AFTER A FEW days it was time to return to Buckingham, so I left Ireland with a hug and a kiss from my mother, who made me promise that I would see the student counselor weekly for therapy and that I would take it easy. Once back in Buckingham, I settled back into my studies and visited the student counselor weekly. The counselor was very nice to me and very sympathetic. She agreed with my mother's recommendation that I needed to attend therapy with her at least once a week and that this, along with the anti-depressant, should cure my depression.

I returned to the normal grind of my getting to lectures on time, studying and preparing for tutorials. As the days went by, I became very sad. My depression was developing a pattern of encroaching on me at three o'clock in the afternoon everyday like clockwork, making me cry for no apparent reason. I did not know why I was crying; all I knew was that I felt very sad inside and nothing I did cheered me up. I tried everything but to no avail. The daily bouts of depression now lasted for about ten minutes.

One day about three o'clock, I was in a lecture when a heaviness slowly came over me, coupled with thoughts of complete helplessness that flooded my mind so that I was overwhelmed with thoughts of failure. I could see no point in studying or in even attending this lecture, and everything seemed too much for me to handle. After this lecture on contract law, I had a criminal law tutorial. Afterwards, I would have to go to the library to read some cases, do some grocery shopping in the evening, and then return home to cook. It was all too much. I could not do it all. Then there was tomorrow when classes would begin at nine o'clock in the morning and I would have to do it all over again. I did not have the strength in me, physically or emotionally to keep up with this race, but all my friends in my class did. They bubbled over with energy and strength, and they never seemed to grow weak or tired. I sat in the lecture and cried. It was all I could do. The best I could do. I had reached my limit.

The days continued like this. Everyday at three o'clock in the afternoon, these feelings would creep up on me slowly and subtly and by quarter past three or twenty past three, the sadness and feelings of hopelessness would be in full swing. By the end of the first week, I had trouble getting out of bed and starting my day. In fact, there were days that I missed lectures because I just could not get out of bed. I tried, but my mind could not deal with the pressures that each day brought and so I found it easier to go back to sleep rather than to face them. The greater the pressures that came with the day, the harder it was to get out of bed and face them. If I had assignments to do that were due that day or a test that day, my mind could not deal with all of these things, and it ran away from them or escaped from having to face them by not wanting to get out of bed. I would sit in bed, and my mind would be plagued by all of the things that I had to do that day. It would just shut down if the day's activities were too stressful. I could not cope and would cry. My memory and mind began to fail me because to avoid dealing with life's pressures; it would just shut down or block out information. After a while the medication contributed to the memory loss as well. This made my ability to function even harder. Now I began to realize that the sadness that came daily at 3:00 p.m. lasted for half an hour and I also realized how punctual it was. At 3:00 p.m. sharp everyday, my emotions went into a slump. I could even set my watch by it, and I began to use its accuracy to make my life a little easier. Wherever I was during the day, I would head for my room as three o'clock was approaching, giving myself ample time to get there. Once there, I would lock myself in, sit in my corner of the room and wait for the depression to hit.

After a while I became accustomed to this routine and learned to live with the condition, the whole time thinking that the problem lay with me. I thought that perhaps I could not handle the pressures that came along with getting a law degree. Well, I adjusted to the condition and lived my life around it. I coped for three to four weeks like this until the duration of the sadness started to increase. In the past few weeks, the *sadness* (as it came to be called) would last for about half an hour, sometimes less but never more. Well out of the blue, it started to increase in length and intensity, sometimes lasting for an hour, then one and a half, until it eventually lasted for two hours. The intensity was also increasing, so the depression would hit me so hard at 3:00p.m that heading to my room at that time was no longer an option but a necessity. It became unbearable. As the months went by, I would sit on the floor in a corner of my room and sob inexorably. Yet I had no reason to be so sad. Sometimes I fell asleep in that corner on the floor because I felt safe being there between two walls—safer than in my bed. Thinking back, that was the real reason why I sat there in the first place. Some nights I would crawl out of bed into my corner on the floor and sleep there. I did not know what was going on in my life, but in that corner I felt safe. I felt I had control over my life again. I ceased going to the library to read cases. I just sat in my little corner on the floor and read the cases that friends had photocopied for me. I was so helpless. I cried to God for help day after day and night after night, but nothing happened. No answer came and no help was given. In fact it seemed that the *sadness* became worse the more I cried out to Jesus for help, so after a while, I stopped crying out altogether. As the days went by, the duration of the depression began to increase. It was going on for more than two hours now—sometimes two and a half, sometimes three—leaving me incapacitated from 3:00 p.m. to 6:00 p.m. every single day from Monday to Sunday. This was my reality, and there was nothing I could do about it.

• • •

THEN ONE DAY, by great providence, I met Mo. I was on my way to a tutorial, and while descending the stairs from the third floor of Pauley House where I lived to the second floor, I heard a loud ruckus coming from the communal kitchen. I went to investigate. There was a lot of laughter, and the joyful noises of people running around chasing each other. When I entered the kitchen, there was Mo chasing one of her friends around, who was trying to avoid being caught. Another girl was sitting at one of the dining tables, bent over laughing at the two of them almost to the point of crying. They were having so much fun. They stopped the chase as soon as they saw me, introduced themselves, and we chatted for a little while. They were each almost a foot taller than I, very slender and very attractive. Each had a figure that would easily grace the top runways of Milan, Paris, or New York. Mo was short for Mojisola Adeniran who came from Lagos, Nigeria. She had very smooth skin, big brown eyes, and full lips. She was very elegant I thought. I was immediately impressed by her physical beauty. She was almost always accompanied by the other two girls who were her closest and dearest friends and who quickly became good friends of mine also. From that day on, Mo became a part of my life because we connected and understood each other. It was practically instantaneous. The girls were all in my year and in the law faculty, and so we all had the same lectures together. Strangely, I did not notice them until during my second semester at Buckingham. Furthermore, they all lived next to each other on the second floor of my building Pauley House, yet still I had not noticed them until today. I was enjoying their pranks and their company so much that I had to force myself to leave their kitchen to get to class on time.

The next morning I was dressing for class when I heard a knock on my door. I opened it, and to my surprise there was Mo. She offered me a lift to class in a taxi that she and the girls had ordered because it was raining. It would be there in a few minutes. I accepted her kind offer, grabbed my books, and we hurried off to meet the cab. It would be almost six weeks later before Mo would divulge to me that Jesus had sent her to my door that morning with the invitation to share the cab.

The next day Mo came to my room to get me for our nine o'clock lecture, but I was having one of those very difficult mornings when my depression was so heavy that I could not get out of bed and face the day. She knocked on the door, and I slowly got out of bed, let her in, and climbed right back into bed again. "I cannot face the day," I told her, not really wanting to discuss my illness. Needless to say, she did not understand my statement. She came in, closed the door behind her, and sat at my desk waiting for an explanation. So I told her about my depression, how it was affecting me, and about the medication I was taking. She was very sympathetic to me. She came over and patted my head like one would do to a puppy. She was going to call the cab company to defer it by about fifteen minutes in order to give me time to shower and dress for class, but I told her to go on without me. I had already spent the last hour and a half–lying in bed awake, trying to get my emotions sufficiently together to face the challenges of the day and had not achieved it, so fifteen minutes more would not make any difference. Mo left reluctantly, and my heart sank as she closed the door behind her. I longed to be with my new friends, but I did not have the strength or energy to even do this. I was so crippled by this thing that it made leading an active lifestyle impossible. It made my energy level constantly low, too low to travel to class and concentrate for a one hour lecture. I took another tablet (the second one in two hours, which is double the recommended dosage) because one tablet was not working, and went to sleep disillusioned and hopeless.

By mid-August, the depression would come on me in the mornings as well as from three o'clock in the afternoon until six or sometimes seven o'clock in the evening. My condition had worsened significantly. I was having weekly sessions with the counselor, who now had to upgrade my medication to the much stronger Prozac. This was such a powerful drug that I awoke each morning with a high about the equivalent of a beer buzz, and this slight euphoric state continued throughout the day. However, after about three months, this drug also lost its effect.

One day Mo came into my room, and I was telling her about my worsening condition and the uselessness of the Prozac. She got very angry at me and said,

"You sound so beaten. You give this thing glory by always talking about it. Don't you know that Jesus can heal you? Instead of asking Him to do so, you talk about your depression all of the time." And with that she stopped in her tracks and held me and apologized for her angry outburst, but it was too late. Her words had already entered my mind and my heart with great force, and I found myself thinking about what she had said and curious as to what she meant by it. So I asked her, to which she responded by telling me that God could do anything. He could heal any disease that man could contract including the ones medicine labeled as incurable; because with God, nothing was impossible. This was something I knew and believed my whole life from age three to my present age, but I did not know how to get Him to do it for me. I asked Him so many times to heal me, but nothing happened. So I stopped asking Him and instead began blaming myself for not having sufficient faith or the necessary requirements that the characters in the Bible had to get their healing.

As the days went by, I began to realize that there was much more to this young Nigerian woman than what met the eye. In fact she did things that had I not seen with my own eyes I would not have believed them. As a rule she never carried an umbrella with her, and she never kept one in her car, which I just could not fathom because with the unpredictable English weather, I considered one a necessity. It was not long before I saw the reason for her unusual habit. One day when we were trapped in an administrative building by torrential rain and we were trying to get to class, I was about to ask her why she did not carry an umbrella, when she just looked up to the sky and the rain immediately stopped. We headed off to class without missing a beat. The first time she did this I silently thought it was purely coincidence, but then she did it again and again and again. By the end of our two year law program, I had seen her do it a total of twenty seven times. I kept count. Sometimes I saw her lips moving, but most times, she just looked up to the heavens as if focusing on someone. All she was doing was asking Him—who was controlling the weather—to stop the rain for her so that she could get to where she was going, and He did it every time. Jesus did it simply because He loved her, she once told me. It was not just limited to rain. I watched her control other aspects of the weather as well. It was December, and meteorologists had predicted it was not going to be cold enough for it to be a white Christmas. I was very disappointed. I had not seen snow since I was five-years-old and living in Ireland, and I desperately wanted to see it fall before I returned to Barbados for the Christmas holidays. So I complained to Mo who promised me that it would snow before I left and that I was not to worry, to disregard the weathermen, and to just leave it to Jesus and her. Needless to say, a few days before I was due to return to Barbados, it snowed. I was elated when I saw it falling that night, and I could not wait until the next morning to go out and play in it. I picked it up and felt it between my fingers. It is a novelty to someone who comes from the Caribbean.

I started to notice how I felt when I was in Mo's room. I went downstairs to her room to study in the evenings after class and on weekends because strangely enough every time I set foot in her room, I felt better. My depression was now at its worst, operating from three o'clock in the afternoon until seven o'clock at night. It would have had me sobbing uncontrollably as I sat in my corner on the floor if I was in my room, but whenever I went down to her room, this did not happen. I felt happier and lighter in her room, and it did not take long before I noticed this pattern. Then one morning, I went to her room earlier than usual to borrow some of her lecture notes, and as she opened the door and as I entered her room, something like rain was falling on me from the ceiling. I felt it hitting my body and my head, but it was not water and it was not wet. There were invisible particles falling from above, and as they fell on me, I immediately felt better. My spirit lifted, I was happy, and my mind and body were energized. She had a CD of black gospel music playing in the background. It was too early in the morning to be playing music, so I asked her what she was doing. She replied that she was worshiping God. So I did not pursue the matter but just took her notes and returned to my room feeling alive and happy. A few days later, she explained that she would sing the songs on the CD to God to worship Him first thing in the morning, and He would respond by letting His power rain down on her. Needless to say, from the next day on, I did not want to impose on her worship, but as soon as she had finished, I would knock on her door and go into her room just to soak in the remnants of rain that were trickling down from the ceiling. This always raised my spirits higher, much higher than the Prozac ever did.

Consequently, I began spending many hours with Mo and her friends. I would be in her room early in the morning to catch the leftovers of the rain, and we would go to all of our lectures together and study in the library together when necessary, but most of our studying was done in her room in the afternoons after classes. I would sit and read or write my notes at her desk while she would write hers seated on her bed. Whatever was in her room made it easier to study and to pass my exams.

Besides all of these strange and amazing phenomena, she was an amazing woman not only because of her supernatural link to Jesus and His willingness to do anything she asked of Him, but also because she was the first true representation of Jesus' love for me that I ever experienced. Here it was that a stranger walked into my life with a flurry of activity and lathered me with love—the likes of which I have never felt before except from my parents and sisters. At first I thought it was ridiculous, but I had no understanding nor had I ever felt Jesus' love for me in a tangible and practical way before. She showered me with so much love that at first I thought it was her love for me, but I realized that He was behind it when it began to be poured out without end, without limit, and with an endurance that withstood even the most difficult circumstances. I soon realized that human love sometimes falters and can weaken in adversity, but God's love does not.

Mo treated me with great respect and love. She brought her car down from London for me to drive in Buckingham. She included me on her insurance policy as a driver, so I could drive to the supermarket and to lectures. She insisted that I do this because it was easier to drive to class with my depression affecting me than it was to walk or catch a taxi. It was simply less of a mental and physical burden. When my depression was very heavy and I did not have the strength to do my own grocery shopping, she would hop into her car and do it for me often spending her money and never accepting repayment regardless of my insistence to do so. After a while as my illness grew worse and I was unable to cook, she shopped and cooked for both of us, and my life was free of this responsibility also. She did this for at least three months of my life. Never before have I been so loved and so grateful for help.

Added to this, her rich Nigerian culture and strong upbringing opened my eyes to a whole new dimension of womanhood that was totally foreign to me. She was like many other Nigerian women who treated men with great respect and honor as if the man was their lord, and their duty was to diligently care for him and tend to him. This made me realize that this woman was any man's dream wife. She cooked for me not only because I was incapacitated and could not cook for myself, but also because she thought it was only correct to do so simply because I was a man and a woman's respect for a man required this. None of the women I had ever met treated men with such respect and care. As I was unaccustomed to being treated like this, it took me quite a while to get used to it. She was very skilled in the kitchen, serving up the best of Nigerian cuisine and stews very similar to what I was accustomed to in Barbados but spicier. She cooked for two days at a time and insisted everyday that I have a hot meal.

• • •

ONE SUNDAY MORNING, Mo was going to her church called the New Life Christian Fellowship Church at ten o'clock, and she invited me. Her church did not meet in a church building but in a school about fifteen minutes walk from Verney Park. It comprised of about twenty five people in all, half of which were English couples from the Buckingham town area and the other half were Nigerian and Bahamian students from my university. When we arrived, they started to sing songs and hymns to God and an abundance of power began to rain down from the ceiling, raising my spirit and making me happy again. It was amazing. Song after song, the power became greater, more intense, and much stronger until I could not stand up any more. I felt weak and sorry for myself, so I sat and wept, having myself a pity party, when suddenly I felt something empower me. It went right through me when I was crying, and I was able to stand up and continue singing. I watched these people sing these songs and hymns with their hands in the air above their heads. I thought it all very strange at first. It took some getting used to. I noticed Mo was worshiping just like the others, and it was beautiful to see all of these people worshiping God in this way. I stood and sang and felt even better. Near the end of the service, they invited anyone who wanted to have a personal relationship with Jesus Christ to come up to the front, and the pastor would lead them in the Sinner's Prayer. I did not know what they meant by a personal relationship with Jesus. What exactly did it entail? All I knew was that it sounded like more work and that I was tired of working. When I heard some people being led in the Sinner's Prayer, I realized that I had been led in it about five years earlier by a Jamaican born-again Christian friend of mine, who I had met while studying sciences at the University of the West Indies in Barbados. So I had already given my life over to Christ, but obviously His effect could not be seen in my life as yet, with things being as bad as they were. The concept of giving my life over to God and letting Him run it was a great idea. At only twenty-six, I was tired of fighting and of the constant, daily, uphill trek that everyone in the world endures—and some even thrive on—calling it progress, self-improvement, and success. There had to be more to life than this. For years I was sure of this, and I was right.

After the service all of the couples came over and introduced themselves. They were warm-hearted people who served coffee and biscuits after the service. They were all just really delightful, and very welcoming.

I could not get over how kind and genuine the people were. I went to this church with Mo every Sunday morning until it was time to return to Barbados for the Christmas holidays.

• • •

IT WAS NOT what I would have expected for the Christmas holidays but to my surprise I returned to Barbados to find my sister, Ranita, running around the house and living an active lifestyle unimpeded and unaffected by any illness. I questioned her about the drastic change, and she said that she was now *born again* and that Jesus had healed her. Since then, she had followed His instructions and had thrown her medication into the garbage. She had told me that when Jesus told her that she was healed, she felt it when He healed her. I listened to what she had to say, but the concept of God speaking to her made me speculative and raised questions in my mind like what did He sound like? Did He have a strong loud voice or a soft gentle one? Whatever had happened—it was obvious that something did take place because she was back to a normal lifestyle, going shopping and going to the gym and to the beach. Her life had returned to normal with one big difference—she had Him. She now attended a Pentecostal Bible study and house church on Saturday evenings instead of Mass on Sundays. A close aunt of ours had been saved a few years before, and she invited Ranita along to the Bible study. Ranita liked it and had been going there ever since.

Without Mo around and the power in her room, my depression jumped into overdrive, and the Prozac was not working anymore. I was at the mercy of the illness from the time I arrived home, and it affected me from twelve noon until seven at night everyday. This was the longest period that it ever affected me. It had never been so bad before. I could not do anything but lie in bed and allow the condition to run rampant throughout my body and my mind. I was helpless against it once again. Mom was very concerned and kept trying to make appointments for me to see a therapist. But I could not even get out of bed before 7 p.m., so how could I keep an appointment which would be sometime in the afternoon? My body became very weak and my memory was failing.

One Saturday morning about two weeks before Christmas day, Ranita came into my bedroom and delivered a message from Jesus, saying, "If you come to Bible study with me today, He will meet you there and touch you and heal you." I was half–dead in terms of energy, and I had given up hoping that God would help me. In fact I was angry at Him for leaving me in this state at the mercy of this thing, and so I did not go. I just rolled over and went back to sleep. The instant I made the decision not to go was when the depression became the heaviest it had ever been on me, much too heavy to push past. Now it lasted for a whole week without lifting once. I did not get relief for even five minutes during that week. It stayed on me every second of every day until the next Saturday arrived. As a result, I spent every day sleeping. That was all I could do. I could not handle any pressure at all. I could not even get out of bed to go outside and get some sunshine. At the age of twenty-six, I was reduced to nothing.

Saturday came around again, and my sister came into my bedroom and delivered a more specific message than the one she had relayed to me previously, "Jesus said to tell you that if you come to Bible study with me today. He will meet you there on the top step, and He will touch you and heal you." Well this time, I was so desperate for help that satan himself could not have stopped me from going to the Bible study. If nothing happened, no one would have been more disappointed than I, but at the time, in my circumstances, I had nothing to lose. Prozac was not helping me neither was Paxil working, Jesus was my only hope. All my eggs were in one basket, and Jesus was that basket. I had never seen miracles like in the Gospels, but I had heard of them from Mo. Well I needed a miracle, or I was going to spend the rest of my life like this. The hard part was that ever since I was a little child I believed and knew that Jesus could do miracles, but lately I was beginning to doubt if He would do one for me. I needed one badly. So this time I made up my mind to go to the Bible study, and as I said, "Yes, I will go" to my sister, the depression hit me even harder. It took all of my physical strength to get out of bed. I had to force myself.

The Bible study started at 4 p.m. and I was out of bed by noon, the earliest I had been up in days. I took a Prozac after lunch, showered, and dressed. Ranita and I left the house at 3:30 p.m. and drove to the Bible study meeting. It dawned on me while driving there that I had not brought a Bible with me, but Ranita assured me that I would not need one. By 3:50 p.m. we arrived at one of the member's homes. It comprised of a small group of twenty five people who met in members' homes instead of in a church building.

We got out of the car, and my sister ran ahead of me into the house, leaving me alone with the challenge of getting up ten little steps that lead onto the patio and to the front door of the house. There was no one on the patio. Everyone was inside singing hymns and songs. I could hear them from the car. I held the handrail and climbed the steps one at a time, and when I reached the top one, I paused to admire the view below me and took a deep breath before entering the house and meeting all of these new people. That was when I heard it. It sounded like a plane falling out of the sky. I looked up skywards into the deep blue heavens to see what was making the sound, and to my utter shock I saw what appeared to be a huge rectangular blanket of hot air falling out of the sky. I could not believe my eyes or my ears. So I closed them and reopened them. But it was still there, and it was falling through the clouds, faster and faster, heading straight for me. It had the appearance and consistency of a large rectangular mirage like when hot air coming off a road meets the cooler air above it, refracting light rays in the process. I was astonished at the size and supernatural consistency of this thing, and I could feel the awesome power it possessed as it was fast approaching. I thought of running away to try and escape from it, but I was incapable of running. It was so large and moving so fast that it was upon me in the blink of an eye. Just a second before impact, I braced myself for the imminent collision...

It hit me, and I felt a tremendous jolt of electricity go through me from my head to my feet like one million volts of electricity coursing up and down throughout my body. It was too powerful, and I stood there trapped in it and held by it with my bones shaking and vibrating under its force and with my body shaking crazily like a leaf in a hurricane. To a spectator, it would have looked like a strong wind was blowing on me from my front. My body was being buffeted by its terrific force causing my hands and arms to shake as if I was having an epileptic episode, and my very bones began to vibrate rapidly. I stood on the top step shaking like a reed in the wind for what seemed like two or three minutes.

What also happened when this power hit me was

that I instantly burst into tears, crying and wailing from the very pit of my being, and no matter what I did, I could not stop. I cried and cried and cried, and the more power that went into me, the more I cried and the better I felt. In the past, I cried but never felt better; this was a change. It must have been a funny sight for an onlooker, with me weeping unceasingly, and at the same time my body shaking uncontrollably under the influence of an unseen, yet powerful wind. This shaking continued for the entire process that took place on the top step until it was over.

When the giant mirage hit me, it also enveloped me with a cloak of tremendous warmth all over my body and my head to the point where my body was becoming hot. The shaking, the crying, and the warmth now went on simultaneously. At which point I heard a voice say, "Keep your eyes open. I want you to see me heal you." Then I looked down at my feet that burned earlier as if I were walking on hot coals but now were cooling down. I looked to see where the coolness was coming from and to my amazement I saw a red line just above my ankles. I quickly shut and reopened my eyes to make sure that I was not dreaming, but the red line was still there. The line began to rise up my body from my ankles to my shins, to my knees, and gradually upwards towards my head. As this was taking place, I realized that the parts of my body above the line were warm, while the parts below the line were very cool.

Then I saw what was causing the coolness. Below the red line there was a cool minty whirlwind which began to blow around my body, encircling it rapidly like a powerful tornado. I could not believe that I was seeing all of this with my own two eyes. *Was this a dream or was it really happening?* I watched the activity of the wind and the red line with my mouth ajar in awe. I soon realized that there was a fight between the two of them for me. The cool wind was chasing the red line and heat out of my body, while the red line wanted to stay. The cool whirlwind was winning, as it was much more powerful than the red line and the heat and for this I was very grateful. As the chase continued, I watched the red line being chased up to my chest, then to my sternum and then to my neck. Finally the whirlwind chased the red line and all the heat from my neck up to my forehead and from there, out of my body. Now all warmth left my body and I was completely encircled by the cool beautiful whirlwind. As the latter part of the battle ensued, I wailed openly and wept buckets of tears uncontrollably and the more I wept the better I felt. However, now that the red line was gone, I was completely encircled by the wind and I stopped crying. I would never cry again. The sadness was gone and it was replaced by incredible happiness. The crying was over and for the first time in six months, I felt genuinely happy on the outside as well as deep down inside myself. I was absolutely elated and completely overjoyed that it was over. My six month bout of sadness had come to an end.

Then I found myself giggling—just giggling and giggling almost stupidly with no real reason for it except for the cool whirlwind that still encircled my body. It brought with it an overwhelming joy that penetrated my pores and infused my body and mind with senseless laughter, genuine happiness, and joy. My giggling turned to laughter, which later turned to raucous laughter which was impossible to stop. I tried to stop, but after realizing that the force of the joy coming from the whirlwind was much too strong for me to subdue, I just let myself go—to laugh freely under the whirlwind's influence and to enjoy it. After all, I had not laughed in six months, and I certainly was enjoying this laughter. I laughed so much and for so long that my sides hurt, and my jaws and cheeks were sore. I laughed uninterrupted for about five minutes, and the laughter was becoming more infectious and more uncontrollable as time progressed. So that at the end of the five minutes, I was laughing so much that I could barely breathe. I could not stop long enough to take a breath of air.

Then all of a sudden, I could hear the people inside singing a song whose words were, "As the deer pants for the water so my souls pants after Thee ..." (Psalm 42:1), and with this, the atmosphere around me suddenly changed, and the cool whirlwind began to breathe strong, quick, short gusts of air into my lungs through my nose. It was a sensation I had never experienced before. It felt like something was resuscitating me and breathing its life into me through my nose with such great force that I could not escape from or stop it. It was such a beautiful sensation that no one would want to escape from it anyway. The whirlwind outside of me was entering into me through my nose and becoming a cool wind inside of me. With each breath I received, I felt more and more satisfied inside and full of whatever this cool wind was. Then even more of this wind began to breathe into me than before, with greater force and even more power so that I was forced to open my mouth to allow it to enter into me and to infill me. So now, I was being infilled through both my mouth and nose. With both orifices open, the whirlwind breathed into me with maximum force—gusts or puffs of wind greater than anything that went before. I was now being pushed back physically. With each powerful breath that was breathed into me, I had to stand firmly on my feet and hold my ground, or else I would have been pushed to the other end of the balcony. The infilling took a total of about one and a half minutes until I could not hold anymore wind in my lungs, and then it stopped. When it ended, I was full inside, and I felt complete for the first time in my life. Whatever this wind was, it had placed a piece of itself in me. The void in the pit of my being was filled up with this wind, and I did not feel empty inside anymore. I felt satisfied, full, and whole for the first time in my life. I was also energized like never before. I felt like I could run a marathon. Finally, I was happy and complete.

I stood on the top step for a while, drying both my face, which was bathed in tears and my shirt, which was tear-soaked to the point that my chest was drenched underneath it. I had never cried so much before. More tears had been shed on the top step in a few minutes than all the tears from the depression over the last six months. *Surely this could not be normal,* I thought to myself.

Then I looked at the trees at the back of the balcony and noticed they were greener. I looked up at the sky, and it was bluer than I had ever seen it before. I looked around and realized that every color was brighter than I had seen it in the past—the reds were redder, the grass was greener, and purple bougainvillea was more purple. *Had everything been given a fresh new coat of paint, or was I given new eyes that saw clearer, crisper and with a higher definition than ever before?* I was seeing things for the very first time. With effortless ease, I stepped into the house and joined the group in singing their songs of worship to Jesus.

• • •

THAT EVENING I went home and watched television until almost one o'clock in the morning—something impossible to do with the depression because it made me tired all of the time and would knock me out by 8:30 p.m. or 9:00 p.m. While I was watching television, something kept singing songs to me. It sang perpetually and would not stop. Even with the television on, it continued to sing and could be heard over the noise of the former. It was singing one of the songs from the Bible study, I recognized the words,

> Give thanks with a grateful heart,
> Give thanks to the Holy One
> Give thanks because He's given Jesus Christ His Son.

It would be a song that would follow me around for many weeks afterwards at every church I visited in Barbados and back in Buckingham.

• • •

THE NEXT MORNING I arose at seven o'clock to the sound of someone singing beautifully. It was the same voice singing the same song to me from the night before. It was then I noticed the bright sunshine outside my window. It was going to be a beautiful warm Sunday morning. What made it even more beautiful was the voice. It spoke to me softly and lovingly all morning. What a beautiful voice it was! The voice reverberated throughout my whole body. It seemed like it was coming from inside of me. (See Ezekiel 36:26–27 and Luke 17:21) I heard it singing to me when I was asleep.

It was the singing that woke me up. I lay in bed for a little while, watching the sun rise through my window and listening to the lovely singing. Whose voice was it? Who was singing, and why did they sing? I sang the song along with the voice and felt wonderfully warm inside. I listened attentively as the voice now began to speak. All it had to say to me was how pleased it was with me and how much it loved me. It was then that I asked it to identify itself. "Tell me who you are?" I beckoned. It responded by singing, what it had sung all morning long,

> Give thanks with a grateful heart,
> Give thanks to the Holy One
> Give thanks because He's given Jesus Christ His Son
> And now let the weak say I am strong
> Let the poor say I am rich
> Because of what the Lord has done for me
> Give thanks.

It was then that I knew that the person speaking and singing to me was none other than Jesus Christ the Son of God. I obeyed what He was telling me to do in the song. I gave thanks. "Thank You Jesus for healing me. Thank You very, very much. I could never repay You for what You have done for me." With that, power fell through the ceiling infilling my lungs through my nose and mouth just like the day before on the top step. The man Jesus Christ of Nazareth who had never ever spoken to me before was now singing to me. This was the first time I had ever heard His voice. Then it hit me like a thunderbolt of revelation. He is alive! He is alive! I knew that He was crucified, died, and was buried and that the apostles gave accounts of seeing His resurrection and visitation of them. Yet I never had any proof. I just accepted that He rose from the dead and that He is alive today, but never did He speak to me or sing to me day after day like this. *Dead men do not speak,* I thought to myself. *They do not sing and they certainly do not touch and heal people of their diseases.* I had proof that He was alive, but I could not share it with anyone. They would think I was crazy. To all those skeptics who questioned His resurrection, arguing that His body may have been stolen from the tomb or hidden by the disciples, I had this answer. He is alive! Jesus is alive! I know this because He woke me up this morning, He sang me to sleep last night, and just like He healed those people in the four gospels two thousand years ago, He healed me yesterday. Nothing has changed. He is still healing people today. He is alive today!

That morning I admired the first sunrise I had seen in six months. I hopped out of bed, changed my clothes, and went for an early morning walk, still giving thanks to Jesus along the way. I helped myself to a hearty breakfast and went outside to play with the dogs. I had not been up so early in the morning in such a long time, and I did not know what to do with myself. I had so much energy, and I was free and happy. There was no more sadness, no difficulty getting out of bed, and no fear of facing the day. Instead, there was a joy inside of me that percolated up through me again and again which never seemed to stop. It was a beautiful morning.

"GEORGE, GEORGE, I LOVE YOU"

THAT SUNDAY NIGHT, I could hear a sweet voice singing the songs from the Bible study. By the time I went to bed, the voice had sung about five different songs. The melodies were sung loudly in my head and would not leave me alone but followed me around everywhere I went. The words were so crystal-clear that—although I had only heard the songs once before at the Bible study—I was able to sing along. *How amazing!* I thought. I have had songs in my head before, but they were my doing and songs I liked and put there. But this was different—something or someone else was singing them in my head. Furthermore, they were not just being sung in my head, but in my chest and all over my body as well so that every cell constituting my body rang out its praise to Jesus.

I went to bed and was awoken by a voice saying, "George, I love you. George, I love you." It said this for a long while, and then it said, "Be baptized George, Be baptized." Every single day, I awoke to the voice persistently saying the same thing over and over again, "Be baptized George, Be baptized." It was a soothing and loving voice, yet the funny thing was that I did not hear it with my ears. It took me a few days before I realized this. The voice reverberated throughout my whole body. It seemed like it was coming from inside of me. (See Ezekiel 36:26–27 Luke 17:21) Again it said, "Be baptized George. Be baptized." Now intermittently—whenever it was not singing—the voice gave me the same command everyday. Sometimes a few times a day, "Be baptized George. Be baptized." It just would not go away but persisted lovingly, ever so gently.

I only had one week of vacation time remaining before classes resumed in Buckingham, that meant that my only opportunity to be baptized in Barbados was from the Sunday morning after my healing and salvation, until the coming Saturday. I was scheduled to depart for Buckingham the following Sunday. I had no problem doing what the voice instructed me to do because it made me feel so secure and confident that somehow I knew the owner of the voice would never let me down. Furthermore, from the way I was feeling inside from the experience on Saturday on the Bible study steps, I would now do anything God asked me to do.

I was so preoccupied with being baptized, that for three days I forgot to take my Prozac. I had not taken Prozac since the day of my healing on the top step, but yet I felt on top of the world. One morning Jesus told me that I would not need the medication anymore and to throw the remainder of the Prozac into the bin. I gladly did so without a care in the world and without fear of a relapse. I felt more alive now than at any other time in my life. I did not need Prozac to lift my spirits because I was already as high as an eagle soaring high above the clouds. Needless to say, I never took Prozac again—ever!

I did not know who would be willing to baptize me or how or where to be baptized. The voice in my mind, belly, and throughout my body told me, "Call Ranita's pastor." So I got his number from her and called him. Realizing that I sounded like a total crackpot, I told him that I would be leaving for England this coming Sunday and that I could hear a loud but beautiful voice telling me over and over to be baptized. He sounded intrigued and asked me what else the voice was telling me to do.

I responded, "There was nothing else except it called me by name on the first morning, and it said it loved me." I also told him about the experience I had on Saturday on the Bible study steps and told him about my depression and how it was now gone and that I felt amazing for the first time in six to seven months.

He listened to my story and said, "Sounds like you got saved, healed, and baptized in the Holy Ghost all on that top step." I did not have a clue what he was talking about, so I did not say anything. Then he said he would pray about baptizing me and would let me know. I asked him what he meant by that, and he replied, "I will ask God about baptizing you, and if He says yes, then I will be more than happy to do so." Well to be honest with you, I had never been so intrigued by anything in all of my life. The thought that God would actually respond to a man's enquiries really impressed me, and I was curious to see what the outcome would be. Besides, I wanted to be baptized so badly that I agreed to his terms. I replied that the arrangement was fine, and the pastor then proceeded to tell me how the baptism would be performed. He always baptized off Mullins Beach on the west coast of the island, which is just five minutes away from his house, and he completely immerses the person's body below the water's surface for a second or two. He asked me if I had a problem with this, and although the concept was completely foreign to me, I said no because there was something inside of me so hungry to do what the voice was telling me to do—that if the pastor had agreed to baptize me at that very moment, I would have willingly allowed him to do so. The conversation ended with his promising to call me as soon as he heard from God.

Within seconds of putting down the phone, I became worried. The voice wants me to be baptized, but now, it depended on what God would tell the pastor to do or not to do. I asked God for help, and immediately the voice that was singing songs of praise to Jesus the Lamb on His Throne every minute of the day unceasingly, assured me saying, "Do not worry, George. Jesus is going to tell the pastor to baptize you, and he will do it this Saturday." With this assurance from the voice, some power fell from above onto me as it did at the Bible study. I was very excited and decided to believe the voice and expect the pastor's answer to be yes.

I told my family about the baptism, and although they were happy for me, they could not understand why I had to be baptized again and to be honest neither did I. I was just following the voice's instructions. I had been baptized as an infant in the Catholic church where the priest sprinkled my head with holy water over a font, and with that, I believed that Jesus washed away my sins and that I would enter into the Kingdom of Heaven when I died. On this basis and with this belief, I had a little difficulty coming to grips with the fact that Jesus wanted me to be baptized again. The only difference being that this time, it would be by the full immersion method. This was strange and new to my family and to me, and so I asked the Father about this full immersion method?

Within seconds, the voice said to me, "If it was good enough for m*y Son*, is it not good enough for you?"

I responded without missing a beat, "Of course it is Father! Of course it is!" I felt a little disappointed in myself for asking the Father what to do when He had already instructed me concerning this. I immediately apologized to Him and determined within myself to follow every instruction He will ever give me beginning with this one. With that, I had an uncontrollable impulse to find a Bible. I had an old one that I used in high school somewhere in my room. I looked for it, found it, and turned to the book of Luke where he wrote about Jesus' baptism by John the Baptist. John the Baptist completely immersed Jesus' body into the River Jordan, and when Jesus came out of the water, the heavens opened, and God the Father spoke saying that this was His beloved Son in whom He was well pleased. The Holy Ghost took the form of a dove and descended upon Jesus. I checked some of the other books—Matthew, Mark and John—and their accounts were more or less the same. It was evident that Jesus had full body immersion and He was the King of Heaven. *So why wouldn't it be good enough for me,* I thought, and I eagerly awaited Saturday.

The next night the pastor called me, and just as the voice had said, he agreed to baptize me the coming Saturday at Mullins Beach. Actually, it was perfectly orchestrated because Bible study was scheduled to be held at his house near to Mullins Beach that Saturday anyway. (Bible study was only held at his house on the first Saturday of the month, so baptisms were only performed on the first Saturday of the month.) The baptism would be at 3:30 p.m., followed by the Bible study at 4:00 p.m. I was very excited and could not wait for Saturday to arrive.

I was grateful that the days went by quickly and that Saturday arrived in the twinkle of an eye. During the whole week, every time I thought about my baptism, I was visited by an atmosphere of excitement and joy that would stay with me for hours on end. This would happen every time I thought about it; without fail, the joy or glee would fill me and the room I was in at the time. When the atmosphere of joy wore off or left, I realized all I had to do to get it back was to just think about Saturday's baptism again, and instantly, it would come right back. I toyed with this phenomenon for a while until I could keep the joy filling the room to full capacity at will, for extended periods of time.

• • •

WHEN SATURDAY FINALLY arrived, I got out of bed with a terrible heaviness upon me. Something or some force was sitting on me like an extra weight on my body, slowing me down and trying to reduce the joy within me. Ever since Jesus touched and healed me and baptized me in the Holy Spirit, I was as high as a kite. My spirit was happy all of the time, and I felt alive and energized everyday. Now this heaviness was trying to reduce this energy, steal this joy from me, and push me back into a depression. I lay in bed until about 1:30 p.m. because the thing on me kept me in a drained and de-energized state. At 1:30 p.m., the heaviness decreased and I rose, showered, and put on a big white t-shirt and my swim suit. I grabbed my beach towel, headed out the door with hugs, kisses, best wishes; and even a present from my mother and Lecia, and hopped into the car with Ranita at the wheel. Destination: the pastor's house.

WHEN WE ARRIVED there, some members of the Bible study were coming out of the pastor's house and were hopping into vehicles to make the two minute drive to the beach. I went up to the house to find the pastor who was outside with his wife and other members of the Bible study. The pastor's wife approached me and said that she had goose bumps all over her body and that she was very excited at what was about to happen. With that she showed me her arms and neck, she was right because she had goose bumps all over, and there was a cool chill in the air. The pastor hopped onto the back of a four-by-four truck that was heading to the beach, and I joined him. It was there that I received my instructions. I would wade into the water with him until it reached me at about chest level. Then, he would hold me from the side and cross my arms over my chest. I would take a deep breath, and he would dip me under the water's surface, holding me there for a second or two before bringing me back up to the surface.

• • •

WE ARRIVED AT Mullins beach, and we headed down to the water's edge. Usually the pastor baptizes a few people at a time, but today there was just one. The twenty five members of the church started to sing songs from the shore. It was a beautiful day, perfect for the beach. The sky was a deep blue, the clouds were white and fluffy, and the calm crystal clear water of the turquoise sea beckoned to me. There were not that many people on the beach at that time, and I was not embarrassed by the twenty-five-strong-voice choir on the shore. I heard someone shout out my name from Mullins Beach Bar where I used to have the occasional drink. There were a few friends of mine there, and they recognized me as I approached the water's edge. I waved at them, then turned, and waded into the water following after the pastor who was a foot taller than I. I grew uncontrollably excited and expectant that something truly amazing was about to happen. Somehow I knew that something was going to happen. I waded behind the pastor who stopped going deeper into the water once the water level reached my chest. He turned me around to face what was now a dancing-and-very-loud choir on the shore, and embarrassment began to creep in. *What were the visitors and other people on the beach thinking,* I thought to myself. The pastor came over to my right side, put my hands together in a steeple prayer position, smiled, and asked, "Are you ready?" I nodded. Then he added quite unceremoniously, "Hold your breath." I took a deep breath, and he tipped me backwards until I was completely covered with water. He held me there for about two and a half seconds, and then he brought me back up to the surface, gave me a hug and congratulated me. We then headed back to the shore where everyone wanted to embrace me and congratulate me. I was given a towel to dry myself and received even more hugs from people who were genuinely happy for me. I could not understand why they were so excited and happy over my being baptized, but they were. They were sincere in their congratulations. Meanwhile three members of the Bible study asked me, "How do you feel?" I did not understand why they were asking me this because I did not feel anything, so that was my reply except for the water being cool and refreshing. I did not know that people felt anything at baptism. I had never heard of anything happening.

The people started to get into their vehicles to return to the pastor's house for the Bible study. I got into the back of the same four-by-four that brought me down to the beach. The pastor and a few little children—most of whom were my nieces and nephews also piled into the back of the pick-up. I sat on the edge of the tray, and as we drove, it began to hit me very slowly like a mild anesthetic. I was slowly beginning to feel very peaceful to the point of it being intoxicating like a sweet smelling anesthetic inhaled prior to surgery. This sweet smelling peacefulness came over me and grew and grew, pervading my entire body and my mind until it had permeated all of me. Time was slowing down as well. It took what felt like ten minutes to drive the two minute journey back to the pastor's house. My little nieces and nephews were playing with my hair, and I could not stop smiling. There was a smile on my face and an overwhelming peace inside of me that seemed to come outwards from inside of me, emanating from every pore of my skin. My sense of hearing was dulled, so all external sounds were muffled. Someone was singing inside of me, and the voice was so beautiful and loud that it drowned out the sound of everything and everyone else around me. I was also as high as a kite. I was in this state of peacefulness alone because no one else could enter into it and share it with me. I do not even think people observing me from the outside realized what I was experiencing inwardly. I wished I could have shared it with someone else.

* * *

WE ARRIVED AT the pastor's house, and we disembarked the truck while the others got out of their vehicles and went up the staircase into the house. I was left alone to climb the nine steps that led to the verandah that nearly encircled his house and the front door. It took me nearly an hour. One hour to climb nine steps. I just kept climbing and climbing and climbing, and the more I climbed, the more I realized that I was punch drunk with love. I had this big smile on my face, and nothing could remove it. It was permanently affixed on me, a reflection of the euphoric state in which I found myself. I was so drunk with God's love that I continued to laugh and giggle uncontrollably. Although intoxicated and by this time, barely able to remain upright, I realized that God had stretched time. Like an accordion, He just expanded the time it would take me to climb these steps, or maybe He increased the number of steps—I am not sure. All I knew was that for the entire duration of my climbing, I always had a step below my feet. I totally enjoyed the experience. I remember laughing as I climbed, climbing as I laughed, and laughing with overwhelming joy too. It seemed that the more I climbed the more I laughed until all the steps were ascended, and I just stood on the balcony, having finally arrived laughing hysterically to the point of crying. I asked the Father why He changed the reality of things so that I had to climb so few steps for so long before I could reach the patio and His response to me was, "So you would not believe what you see with your eyes but only believe what I say, because I am able to change the physical reality of things from the way they appear to what I say they are."

I walked over to a patio chair facing the setting sun. That was when I noticed that I was not walking on the tiled floor but on what felt like a cushion of air approximately one centimeter above the ground. I felt as light as a feather in my spirit, and my body itself felt lighter. So light in fact that I could not feel the usual weight of my body on my feet because now there was less weight on my feet. I had become lighter and did not know how. I sat in the seat and looked out at the gorgeous pink and orange sky and the setting sun, and all I could hear was the voice singing that Jesus' blood washed my sins away and this explained the lightness of my body. It was because I was carrying around only my body weight without the sin. With my sins washed away, I was not carrying them around with me anymore like I had done all my life, and as a result, I experienced physical lightness.

Something or someone was explaining these things to me very clearly, and it sang and sang as I sat watching the beautiful sunset. I watched it for about an hour before falling asleep, amazed at the events of the day and not wanting it to end because it was such a gloriously amazing day. My sister woke me about three hours later. It was time to go home. I had missed the whole Bible study, the worship, and the message, but that was all right because I had tasted something much, much more valuable—"His peace that transcends all understanding" that I never thought would be so powerful and that was greatly needed in my life.

• • •

THE NEXT DAY was a Sunday, and I was awakened by the sound of a voice calling my name saying, "George. George. Wake up. George, I love you." Over and over I heard this unmistakable voice in my sleep, and when I awoke, I could still hear it. My family's house was a large three story upside down house. It was built going down a steep hill, so they parked their cars in the garage on the top floor through which they entered the front door and descended a staircase to the second floor and likewise to the third floor. My bedroom was on the second floor while everyone else's room, my parents' and my sisters' were on the first or top floor as well as the other rooms of the house—the kitchen, the sitting room, and the dining room. In fact my parents' bedroom is directly above my own. So when I heard someone calling me, I assumed it was my mother calling me for Sunday breakfast, which was a traditional English breakfast of sausages, bacon, scrambled eggs, and toast. Being famished, I scooted up the stairs—skipping up them two and even three at a time—all the way to the first floor, and I darted into the kitchen, but to my dismay there was nobody there. In fact the whole house was still locked up, the windows were still locked from the night before, and so, being very disappointed I quietly returned to my room where I climbed back into bed and resumed sleep. Within minutes I heard a beautiful and loud voice calling me again, "George, George wake up," and as before I awoke and darted up the stairs to the kitchen. But once again, there was no one there. The kitchen windows were still closed, and nothing had been prepared or cooked in the kitchen. I checked the adjacent dining room, but there also—all the windows were still locked up. I walked into my parents' bedroom only to see them fast asleep, and I wandered back down to my room on the second floor, thinking that the voice was part of a dream. I was puzzled, but one thing I realized was that my body was energized by this voice. My skin and the blood in my veins echoed and resonated to the sound of this voice. I could feel this happening in me on each of the two occasions that I heard the voice, but I just put it down to adrenaline or a dream. I looked at the clock in the dining room. It was five minutes to six in the morning, and I thought to myself that Mom does not usually rise until about nine o'clock or later on Sundays. So I returned to my room, got into bed, pulled up the covers, and went back to sleep, when five or six minutes later I heard the voice again, "George ... George ... I love you. George ... George ... I love you. George ... George ... I love you. Georgie ... wakey, wakey! George, please wake up." This time I was startled when I awoke because I could not just hear the voice, but I could feel the emotions of the speaker of the voice when it spoke and as it pleaded with me to wake up.

I could feel how badly it wanted me awake and how it wanted to spend time with me because it was pleading from its heart that tugged and pulled at my heart strings until I sat up in bed and asked the voice that was speaking to me, "Who are you?" Then all of a sudden I saw it. In the right hand corner of my room next to the dresser, was a radiating power that was so beautifully joyous and yet it filled me with awe. I felt like it would burn or consume the very skin off my bones. So I leaped off the side of the bed and hid behind it, using the bed between us for cover. Although I hid behind the bed, the room was filled with a cool thick dense mist like atmosphere of indescribable joy, and a cool wind kept circulating in the room. I was not afraid of it. I was just amazed at what I was witnessing. I peeped up over the top of my bed and saw it. There was a person standing about seven feet tall with the figure and shape of a man cloaked in a gloriously bright gown, radiating His glorious power and joy everywhere. He was looking right at me and smiling.

I asked Him, "Who or what are you?"

"I Am the God of Abraham, Isaac and Jacob..."

He looked me square in the eyes and replied, "I am the God of Abraham, Isaac, and Jacob, and I will be your God too if you let me." He stood there with all of His glory on, radiating such an abundance of power and overwhelming joy that my jaw dropped in awe.

I stood up with my eyes riveted in the direction from which His glory radiated and emanated until it filled the room. It was wonderful, like Heaven itself. There was joy everywhere. It dripped from the ceiling and down the walls, it filled my heart to a bursting point, and I found myself very excited and extremely happy—beyond any happiness I had ever felt in my life before. Such beautiful joy surrounded me that I knew this is what Heaven must be like. I have never known such joy before nor did I even know it existed. Part of me could not believe this was happening, yet all of me was comfortable to bask in His beautifully joyous Presence. I could hear Him speak clearly and loudly, yet I did not hear Him with my ears. But it seemed that all of my body heard Him or rather something inside my body heard Him. He began to speak.

He reminded me that when I was nine–years–old and was an acolyte at St. Dominic's Roman Catholic Church I had read a book in Sister Therese's library on Moses liberating the Israelites from Egypt. I was angry at God because He would not appear to me and talk to me like He did to Moses—even though I served Him as an acolyte every single Sunday from age eight to nine. He remembered this saga and how I showed my discontent with God by not serving Him on the altar for two Sundays but instead stayed in the congregation. (This was unheard of for me because I loved to serve God as an acolyte, and from age eight to twenty six I never missed a Sunday except for this particular occasion. In my limited understanding, I believed this was a way to please God, and so I always wanted to do it.) God had remembered every detail of this, and although it happened when I was nine years old and now I was twenty six, He was answering my request. He told me that He never forgets. He remembered my argument to Him that went like, "Moses loved you, and I love you. So, why would you appear and speak to him but not to me?" Now He was appearing to me and speaking to me face to face because I was now born of the Spirit, and without that, this type of communication would be impossible. He turned down His glory, which I realized He could do at will. Then He came closer to me, sat on the edge of my bed, and proceeded to tell me about all the times that were painful and lonely in my life. There were many. He knew every single one and assured me that He was with me through every one. He knew the name of every girl who had ever broken my heart and how I had asked Him to remove the pain and hurt that caused my broken-heartedness. As He spoke, the faces of the girls flashed through my mind like a slide show. He knew the days and nights when my depression was so bad that I would lock myself in my dorm at university and sit in my little corner of the room because I could not handle being around anyone. I would be crying to Him for help to take away my sadness that was overwhelming and overpowering for six months of my life. He sat at the bottom of my bed and spoke for three hours—from six o'clock to nine o'clock in the morning—of all the sad times in my life when I needed Him to comfort me. He reassured me that He was there on every occasion for the entire duration of my pain.

It was uncanny the details He knew and the things He remembered, especially when I was the only one in the circumstances and the only witness to these hard times. The fact that He knew every detail of the events and my feelings at the time meant that this invisible God was there too. Of one thing I am certain, no other human was there.

So He talked, and I listened for about three hours after which He left the room by just fizzling out of view. He just disappeared before my eyes just as quietly as He had appeared and just as my mother began calling me for breakfast. This time it was her voice, and I ran upstairs for breakfast. I was starving.

I AM CHOSEN

IT WAS FEBRUARY 1971, and Belfast was in the midst of turmoil. The British Government had declared a 6 p.m. curfew, which the Royal Ulster Constabulary (RUC), backed by the British Army, were enforcing. No one was to be on the streets after 6 p.m., whether on foot or driving a vehicle. The public was warned over and over again that if anyone broke the curfew, the army would shoot first and ask questions later. The purpose of the curfew was an attempt by the British government to curtail a recently stepped up campaign of violence by the Irish Republican Army (IRA) against Unionists (citizens loyal to the British Government), the RUC and the British military. Only six months before, riots had broken out when Orange Apprentice Boys (Nationalists) held a parade in Derry, and one thousand police (RUC) were called in to contain the crowd. A few days later, the British government sent troops into Belfast to maintain order. Things went steadily downhill after that. It became an almost daily exercise of "an eye for an eye" and a "tooth for a tooth" from both sides. There were reprisals by nationalists and the IRA and counter-reprisals by the loyalists, and so it went on day after day and night after night. The Provisional IRA, who later came to be known as the *Provos,* was born at this time. They split from the original IRA and were the driving force behind the nationalists, leading a campaign of bombings and shootings to get the British out of Ireland and their country one step closer to self-government. The British government counteracted by implementing the curfew and having soldiers patrol the streets at night. Every now and then, one could hear the bombs going off, but even more often, there was the sound of sporadic gunfire. The IRA was using the curfew to their advantage, lying in wait and shooting at any vehicles passing by. The rationale being that since only the police and the soldiers were supposed to be on the streets after 6 p.m., all vehicles were presumed to be driven by them. There was, therefore, no need for the IRA to exercise due care to positively identify their targets as government forces before opening fire. They could simply shoot at a vehicle or blow it up with fair certainty that its occupants were soldiers or the RUC. The locals were not breaking the curfew especially in these dire circumstances. Belfast was experiencing the worst spate of bombings and bloodshed since the Anglo-Irish War of Independence. It seemed a flagrant misuse of the English language and a terrible understatement to refer to the bombings, shootings, and riots of this time as *the Troubles,* but that was what the Irish were calling them. The IRA were detonating bombs in the city center and confronting the RUC in the streets with anything from rocket propelled grenades and machine guns to homemade Molotov cocktails. The locals tried to ignore the volatile situation that was all around them and to get on with their lives, but this was just not possible.

In the midst of all of this Dr. Shirley Jhagroo was pregnant with her firstborn and was concerned about a few things. First of all, she and her husband Dr. Walter Jhagroo worked in the Royal Maternity Hospital on Grovenor Road, and as such, they were given a house to live in—located in a street just opposite the hospital called Crumlin Road. Although tremendously convenient, this arrangement turned out to be a disaster. It was a badly war-torn area because Catholics lived on one side of the road and Protestants on the other, so there were numerous shootings in the street very near to their house. The Jhagroos could hear the deafeningly loud gunfire of machine guns just outside their house. British soldiers and RUC officers were being gunned down by the IRA—and vice versa—just outside their windows and front door, and the screams of anger and fear could be heard every night, night after night. The war was at its worst in July 1970, and the fighting in the neighborhood had reached the worst it had ever been. Prior to this, the Jhagroo family would only hear the occasional stray bullet zip through the air and hit the outside of the house where it would often become lodged. Now things were much worse. Such occurrences happened much more frequently, leaving as a testimony a pattern of holes in the sides of the house visible by any passerby. This frightened the Jhagroos, but it was not easy to look for another house with Shirley pregnant and Walter being on call most of the time. Then one night while they were asleep, a bullet entered the dining room and got lodged in the wall beside the dining table just next to a window frame causing the glass to shatter. They awoke in the middle of the night to the sound of shattering glass as the remnants of the pane hit the floor. This was the last straw. It was the first time a bullet had entered the house. Within a few days Shirley's older brothers Hughley and Roy, who were visiting at the time, went in search of a house to rent, which they soon found in Ormeau Road. Ideally, the couple wanted a house that was near to the hospital but in a safer area. Their new home met these requirements.

A few months later on February 9, 1971, I was born at the Royal Maternity Hospital on Grovener Road and was placed in the arms of my grandparents who had flown all the way from Guyana, South America just for my birth. The war had reached its peak and was at its absolute worst at this time. Grovener Road was a badly war–torn area because Catholics lived on one side of the road and Protestants on the other; and ever so often, there would be a clash in the street between the two, or a shot would ring out, fired from across the street. It was a regular occurrence that British soldiers were called in to quell the unrest. Sadly members of both sides and the army died there also. Despite all of this, Grovener Road was still a safer and quieter neighborhood than Crumlin. This was the setting outside the *Royal* just as I was being delivered by caesarean section.

• • •

MY NAME IS George Girjanand Jhagroo, and I was the firstborn and only son to Dr. Walter and Dr. Shirley Jhagroo. My father is an ear, nose, and throat surgeon and my mother is an obstetrician and gynecologist. My family has a long tradition of excellence when it comes to education that is evident by the large number of cousins, uncles, and aunts who went to Northern Ireland and England to study either medicine or law. They are too numerous to mention, but the number of doctors and surgeons produced in the three generations from my grandfather's generation down to mine almost doubled the number of barristers. In keeping with this tradition, my younger sister, Ranita, left home to study medicine in Belfast, Northern Ireland while Lecia, my youngest sister, went to Leeds, England to study dentistry. It was thought that I would follow in my mother's footsteps and become a gynecologist, and for a while things seemed to be going that way. I studied sciences in high school all the way up to A-levels; however, I disliked chemistry and was no good at it. Since it is impossible to study medicine without chemistry, my hopes of ever becoming a doctor were dashed. Soon afterwards, the legal profession caught my attention, and I chose to study law. I attained my Bachelor of Arts degree and Master of Laws degree from the University of Buckingham. However, while studying for my undergraduate degree, I discovered that I was made for something else, something far beyond anything I could ever have imagined. The revelation made almost everything that happened in my life that led up to that point almost of no value.

• • •

MY MOTHER SPENT most of her life growing up in New Amsterdam, the town of the county of Berbice in Guyana while Dad lived in Village number sixty in an area called the Corentyne (pronounced = Curr-an-teen). Here the villages were numbered from one to sixty nine, and Village number sixty was almost a two hour drive away from where my mother lived. My parents attended the same high school called Berbice High School and became sweethearts, which they remained throughout their high school years. My mother's friends consistently teased her about my father saying, "Walter, Walter, take me to the altar, altar!" which she found very annoying. They separated when they left Guyana to study medicine. My mother went to Queens University in Belfast, Northern Ireland and my father to Velore Christian Medical College in Madras, India. But they kept in touch writing to each other for the five years that they were apart. My father was in India continuously unable to return home until his studies were completed. After they both completed their undergraduate degrees in 1969, they returned to Guyana to be married, and in 1970 they returned to Belfast together to do their postgraduate studies. I was born a year later. We remained there for two years during which time my father also studied at the Royal College of Surgeons of Edinburgh and returned to Belfast. In 1973 they immigrated south of the Emerald Isle to Dublin where my sister Ranita was born, only to return to Belfast in 1975 for Lecia the youngest to be born. At the end of this five year period in Ireland, all of their postgraduate degrees were attained, and my parents returned to Guyana to live. However, we only lived there for two years before my grandfather, George (my mother's father) strongly advised my parents to leave the country. He foresaw that there was trouble on the horizon many months before it happened.

The country would soon pass its leadership over to Forbes Burnham and the PNC government, (People's National Congress), resulting in drastic changes that would cause such a rapid decline in the economy of the country—that to this day—it has not recovered. *Burnham*—as he quickly came to be known—single handedly caused the Guyanese people to suffer for many years by prohibiting all regional and international imports into the country and promoting self-sufficiency in an effort to cut expenses and build the nation's revenues. This meant rationing electricity, gasoline, and water and even banning the importation and use of basic necessities for survival such as flour (made from wheat), sardines, potatoes, and powdered milk to name a few. Locals had to eat bread made from cassava and feed their babies on cow's milk, which was too heavy for them to digest. On the whole, it was a time when people did what they had to do in order to survive.

Months before this became reality, my parents heeded my grandfather's warning and immigrated to Trinidad where we lived for two years in St. Ann's Gardens in the capital of Port-of-Spain. After which time, my father was offered the post of head of the ear, nose, and throat department at the Queen Elizabeth Hospital in Barbados. So we moved to Barbados in 1982, and it became our home and has remained so ever since. My family was saved from a life of hardship just because we heeded and obeyed my grandfather's advice. His advice was always correct. Any one of his children would tell you this. It was as though he could walk forward to the edge of time, take a glimpse of the future, return to the present, and adjust his life accordingly to accommodate what he saw was coming. I did not understand how he did it, but he became well–known among his friends for giving very sound advice. He was almost never wrong.

It turns out that this man, whom I called affectionately only as *Grandfather*, was no ordinary man. There were signs of this which I observed as a child growing up, but as I was ignorant of identifying the fruits of the Kingdom of Heaven at the time, I did not recognize them for what they actually were. He was single–handedly responsible for starting me out on the right track in the perfect will of God at the very beginning of my life, for which I am eternally grateful but more on that later. Aside from having the uncanny ability of knowing what to do about things that were yet to happen in the future, he was very warmhearted, sincere, and caring. He was a very compassionate man who shared and felt people's hardships as though they were his own. I remember walking beside him as a little boy and witnessing him putting aside money in his pocket for beggars who were known to frequent the areas where he walked. Unlike everyone else—who would give small, almost insignificant amounts—he kept fairly substantial amounts of money just for these people in his pocket as long as he could afford it. I have seen him give money and food to the homeless on the streets and remind my grandmother to instruct the cook once a week, year after year to prepare food for the hungry and homeless who arrived expectantly, forming long lines at their doorstep. By the time Grandfather was in his mid-fifties, he was a millionaire on account of following one good business idea after another. But this did not change him, for he continued to have a heart for the poor and the destitute. It was no wonder everyone liked him. I know my little heart was filled with admiration for him.

As a young boy growing up, I heard stories from my uncles and my grandfather's friends about the rags–to–riches story of my grandfather. About how he had amazing business ideas and how he made them one by one into reality. Grandfather's business ideas made him a very wealthy man in a short space of time and the more he instituted his business ideas the wealthier he became. I often wondered as to what was the source of his ideas, but now I know that all along they were God's ideas and that He communicated them to Grandfather as he went through life. My grandparents owned a store and originally sold haberdashery from which they made their livelihood. However, Grandfather started putting his ideas into play and began varying his usual business stock to include beautiful mattresses, beds, and headboards. He also branched out into the grocery business obtaining government contracts to provide the government hospital and prison with fresh fruits, vegetables, and groceries. Later on, he would invent a new system of payment, which he called *Balance Parcel.* It was very similar to the layaway plan that is used today by modern department stores, but the idea belonged to Grandfather. He began using it years before the big department stores in Georgetown thought about it.

So here was my grandfather exhibiting the fruits of the Spirit for all to see such as foreseeing future events or being warned of them, having compassion for the destitute and homeless, feeding them on a regular basis and giving them money when they asked for it, and instituting the ideas that God gave him and becoming very wealthy as a result. He soon became a millionaire, and one of the wealthiest men in Georgetown. However, as I was unsaved up to the time of his passing, I could not discern these traits for what they actually were. It was not until after I experienced salvation eleven years after his passing that my eyes were opened and I realized that my grandfather was in fact saved. I had seen him demonstrate the fruits of the Holy Ghost from the time of my birth, but now I had questions such as when did he experience salvation and how did it happen? It was not until writing this chapter that Jesus began to reveal the answers to me.

WHEN MY MOTHER'S brother Roy was seven–years–old, he developed osteomyelitis of the knee, which is inflammation of the bone, and so he ran the risk of becoming septic all over his body or losing the ability to walk. The doctors wanted to remove his leg to prevent the condition spreading to other parts of his body. My grandparents were horrified at the thought of the surgeons' doing this, but if it was necessary to save his life, they would have no choice but to allow them to amputate. As the family was Presbyterian, they asked a Presbyterian minister to come to the hospital and pray for their son before he went in for surgery, but he never arrived. They sent message after message, but still there was no sign of him. The minister sent a message back explaining that he could not leave what he was doing. Roy was scheduled to go into surgery in a few minutes, and my grandparents wanted a priest to pray for him and to perform last rites in the event that he did not survive the surgery. The family was desperate and went in search of any minister or priest who could pray for Roy and perform last rights if necessary. It took my mother all of three minutes to find a Catholic priest in the Catholic hospital where Roy was admitted called the Sisters of Mercy Hospital.

The priest was very willing and ready to pray for Roy and gave him his last rites. My grandfather believed that God was a good God and that He would understand the plight of his son in these circumstances. He was sure that God would not mind the petition and prayers of a Catholic priest instead of a Presbyterian minister in such desperate circumstances; after all they are all Christian.

Miraculously, Roy's plight began to improve after the priest prayed for him. During surgery, the doctors who had previously advocated amputating his leg—now all of a sudden—were against doing so and instead drained the inflammation from the bone. The family was grateful for the positive turn of events. However, what impressed them more was the countless days the priest stood by them at Roy's bedside and supported them when they needed it most. For the entire nine month period that Roy was in hospital, the priest was by his bedside. Day after day, he was there. There were times that people sent for him, but he just replied saying that he could not leave. He had a genuine liking for the family as well as a sincere hope for Roy's recovery, and it only took a few days before the feeling was mutual and reciprocated by the family.

Within a few months, Roy was sitting up in bed, talking, laughing, and feeling just like his old self again, but it would be a year before he would walk again. Even with regard to this, the doctors were unsure as to whether he would ever walk again, but with more prayers from the priest, he was walking within a year. Within months of Roy's recovery, my grandparents and their three sons converted to Roman Catholicism and were baptized into the faith. From those days to the present, it is unheard of my parents or any of my mother's three brothers' families ever missing Sunday Mass. My grandfather clung to his newly–found faith with both hands and never let go.

• • •

YEARS AFTER I was saved and my grandfather had passed away, the Holy Ghost gave me the vision countless times, that when I was very young sometime before my second birthday, he was lulling me to sleep on his lap, one night in his Berbice chair. My parents had returned from Ireland to spend a few weeks in Guyana and had gone out for the evening, leaving me in the care of my grandparents. However, my grandmother was not in the room, she was taking a shower, leaving me alone with Grandfather in the living room. But we were not alone. A dense cloud had formed around my grandfather and spread out until it filled the room. There was a cool wind blowing through the living room, almost chilly, and there was joy in the air like there is at Christmastime. In the vision, my grandfather was talking to the Lord and telling Him how much he loved Him saying that he was going to live up to the promise he had made many months before, that he would give Him one of his grandchildren as a gift. He affirmed that the child in his arms was the one that God had chosen. Then shakily, he rose from his Berbice chair, trembling amidst the cold, dense cloud and gingerly bore me up in his arms above his head and raised my little body up toward Heaven. With his arms shaking and with tears streaming down his cheeks, I was presented to God, given as a gift to Him with no strings attached. That was my presentation. (A few months before this I was christened in the Catholic Church and given my grandfather's name). Imagine being named after my presenter, my grandfather George a few months before my presentation. At that tender moment of offering this child to God, the Father's heart was undone. My grandfather, who did not know Jesus Christ personally, had not asked God for anything in return. He simply loved God and wanted to express that love to Him in any way he could.

At that moment God looked upon the sincerity of his heart and my grandfather found favor with God, and He smiled upon him. God began to speak, "Thou good and faithful servant because you have a pure heart towards me and desire nothing from me in exchange but to love me, I will give you a gift also, which you have not asked for but which is the most precious and priceless gift, as it was bought for you with the blood of my Son." With these words, the cool wind that surrounded my grandfather as he bore me up unto God, now became stronger and cooler, and power fell from the heavens through the ceiling into my grandfather who stood there shaking and weeping like a reed in the wind. He was being infilled by this wind and could not help but inhale quickly with sharp, short breaths as God breathed His life into his mortal body. This went on for a few seconds, almost a whole minute, and with that, my grandfather was saved. Salvation was given to him at that moment as a free gift, a gratuity not in exchange for anything, not earned, and not even asked for. Now he could dwell with the Father for all eternity after his passing.

Tears covered his face, and joy filled his heart. He was smiling and laughing as he lowered my little body back down to shoulder level and cradled me in his arms. He remained standing because he knew that God was still in the room. He laughed and talked with God for quite a long while that night, able to converse clearly with his Master, and to hear God speak audibly to him for the first time ever in his life. They fellowshipped together, he and this cool wind for almost an hour before my grandmother arrived to put me into my cot.

I realize now in hindsight that I am the second generation in my family to be given the privilege to fellowship with the Holy Ghost manifested in bodily form and to have Him on a regular basis; my grandfather being the first. Once I asked the Lord how my grandfather chose which child to give to Him. He replied that he did not do the choosing. God did. It was God who chose me to be His gift. It was He who chose me for Himself. I have been given this vision many times, and each time I questioned the Lord about it, He reassured me that my grandfather gave me to Him. Who had showed him which child God had chosen remained a mystery to me for a long time. Today I know it was the beautiful Person of the Holy Ghost.

SISTER MARY THERESE OF ST. ANGELA'S SCHOOL

Our First Meetings

SOON AFTER MY family moved to Barbados, I attended Saint Angela's School, which was run by the Sisters of the Ursuline Convent. One of them had a tremendous impact on my life, to whom I am forever indebted. Her name was Sister Mary Therese. She came to Barbados from Canada, and she taught singing and religious knowledge to my class. She was the first firm foundation of the Gospel of Jesus Christ to me, and what a foundation it was. Yes she was my religious–

knowledge teacher, but I learned more about Jesus by the way she lived, the things that Jesus told her, and an ever–present cool wind which surrounded her from day to day, but more on that later.

In my first three years of school from age eight to eleven, she taught me singing. My voice was a medium–pitched, unfluctuating one, and I could not sing the notes but only talk along to the words of the songs. However, singing was my favorite class. The whole school of kids would sit every Friday afternoon and sing children's songs to Jesus, and I wished I could sing like them. Little by little, ever so slowly, and over the space of two years, Sister Therese shaped and molded my voice to hit just about any note she wanted me to, and I did not even realize what she was doing. Although I had perfect pitch, I had to strain and to endure some discomfort in my throat to hit the notes. Almost every Friday for one year, I asked Jesus to make it easier and painless to sing the songs, and then one Friday afternoon during singing class, I felt something move in my throat, in the region where my Adam's apple would appear a few years later. It was a sudden, yet gentle movement, and I quickly felt my throat. There seemed to be no physically detectable difference, but when I resumed singing, to my utter surprise I found that I did not have to strain anymore to hit the notes, and the sound that was produced was beautiful. The sounds were being produced almost effortlessly. I was so grateful that I was brought to tears. I just sat there crying and thanking Jesus for what He had just done to my voice. That day I sang and sang and sang. I sang my little heart out to Jesus. From that day onwards, I sang at home, in the bath, and everywhere, and then a few weeks later, Sister Therese asked me to play the lead role of Joseph—a part which required singing many solos in front of the whole school and their families in the Christmas play. God had only just given me a singing voice, but I was eager to test it out. Besides, I was honored to be given the role and did not want to let Sister Therese down.

More important than singing, Sister Therese represented a true servant of Jesus to me because He spoke to her. He spoke to her regularly, and I was very impressed by it. By age nine, she had me in awe when she told me that Jesus spoke to her concerning me.

"What did He say?" I implored eagerly.

"He said that you will be a priest." She replied confidently and with completion. I was royally impressed. The mere fact that Jesus spoke to her got my attention. A few times, He told her this, and each time the message was always the same—that one day I would be a priest. The news spread like wildfire throughout the convent so that most of the nuns came to know who I was and what Jesus said concerning me. Within days they gave me the nickname the *Little Bishop,* which was further enhanced by the fact that I became an acolyte at St. Dominic's Church around this time, and the nuns saw this as the fulfillment of the early stages of becoming a priest. At the time, both the nuns and I were under the impression that I would become a Catholic priest, and I geared myself in this direction for quite awhile. Little did I know the surprise that I would be in for many years later.

The more she spoke about Jesus and about what was on His mind each day, the more I sensed that God was always present in the library where she spent most of her time as the school librarian. There was a cool wind that would blow through the library, leaving the air filled with joy and excitement. He seemed to follow her around, so whenever she was there, He was there also. Time after time, I would be sitting in the library with the other little children on the floor, and I would begin to feel a coolness in the room that filled it completely. In fact, the library never got hot and sticky even under the hot midday sun.

Then one morning, I was standing outside the library, lining up with the rest of the children down the staircase, waiting for Sister Therese to come and unlock the door and let us in, when I started to feel this cool breeze blowing around all of us in the line. If I did not know better, I would have thought that He was in there waiting for her to come and open up the library. It was as though He was waiting for her to come to Him. I had goose bumps all over me, and I enjoyed the sensation so much that I did not want it to end. I closed my eyes and savored it, cherishing every moment of it. As I did this, I began to feel a nervous excitement growing within me like butterflies fluttering around in my stomach. My body began shaking and vibrating while I stood in the line at the excitement of what was awaiting me inside the library. It was almost as though He lived in there because she spent many hours working in there every day. He was there because she was there. As Sister Therese climbed up the staircase towards the library, the vibrating in my body increased and could be felt in every one of my bones as could the excitement within me. I just savored it all and entered the library along with the rest of the class.

Inside, the joy was everywhere. It was like Christmas Eve. It was such a beautiful atmosphere that it brought tears to my eyes. I could not stop crying, and I did not know why. I was not at all sad in anyway; on the contrary, I was very happy. It was a wonderful yet puzzling experience, and it would be years before I would understand what actually transpired.

It was only later on when I became a little older that I found out that He loved Sister Therese, that she loved Him, and that He walked with her to ease her loneliness. One day she shared with me something very personal to her. She told me that when she was a little girl no more than six–years–old, she received her calling. Jesus appeared to her in a dream, asked her to teach little children about Him, and how to sing to Him. She promised Him that she would do so, and so her fate was sealed. Everyone in her family loved music. They all sang on a daily basis including her father, and some of them played instruments. There was always someone making music in her household, so teaching even the worst tone–deaf child how to sing was easy for her. She loved Jesus and music, so she would spend her life spending time with Him and doing the thing she loved most in life. When she became of age, she entered the nunnery and took her vows. She was posted to various Caribbean islands, and Barbados was one of them. Unfortunately, she found some of her days in the convent very lonely, and her solution was to ask Jesus to accompany her wherever she went. As for when this began to happen, I do not actually know. It seemed to be going on from the first time I met her. She told me that she chatted with Him in the dark lonely halls of the convent, and that He walked beside her hand in hand day after day. They were together in the chapel, in her quarters, in the garden, everywhere. He could be felt walking beside her wherever she went.

I remember the first time I felt Him around her. She was walking down the covered way, a long sheltered path that linked the whole school like a highway. I was about nine–years–old, and I was playing with some friends and saw her coming. I loved her because she always made a fuss of me. The other children were afraid of her, but not I, she doted on me. I saw her coming down the covered way and ran to greet her while my friends ran away "Hello Sister Therese. How are you?" I asked still running to her. She raised her bushy–blond eyebrows at me that were now graying and smiled with a twinkle in her eyes. Everyone knew what this meant and that she was excited about something or that something wonderful had happened and she was about to tell you about it. So I braced myself for it.

"I am fine my *Little Bishop,* and how are you?" she asked.

"I am fine. Is there anything I can do for you?" I replied.

"I just left the library. A new shipment of books has just come in, and I was organizing them. There are some very nice ones. You should pop by later and see which ones you would like to borrow." There was that twinkle in her eyes again that meant she knew something that I did not. I wondered what it could be, but I did not ponder it for long because I felt God lingering around her. He was like the coolness and excitement that is found lingering in the air at Christmastime. This was a feeling I absolutely loved as did most children my age. I loved being around her just to feel Him. I loved the joy that accompanied Him. I could never get enough of it.

"Oh dear!" she exclaimed "I seemed to have forgotten one of the books in the library. Would you be a good child and go up to the library for me? Take this key, open the door, go inside and bring me the book that is lying flat on the shelf next to my chair. Only bring that book and no other. It is the only one lying flat all the others are on their side on the shelf. If you would bring the book back to me, I would be very grateful. I need it for a class I am going to teach after lunch. I am not as young as I used to be, and the stairs are not kind to my knees anymore." She laughed to herself.

"Yes Sister." I responded, and with that I took the keys and ran into the St. Joseph building which housed the library.

I ran up the flight of stairs to the library and remained standing outside the library door window looking in. Within a few seconds, I began to feel the cool wind again. My little bones shivered and shook with the eager anticipation of Whom or what lay beyond the door. I quivered as the cool wind got even stronger as I inserted the key into the lock. All of the hair on the back of my neck now stood perfectly erect and ready at attention. With one turn of the key, I opened the door.

All of the windows were firmly shut, the room was very dark, but I was not afraid. There was joy in the room. I reached over, flicked the switch turning on the lights, and closed the door behind me. I knew that I was not alone in this place, and I began to walk around looking at the numerous books on the shelves. The cool wind was everywhere now, and it was getting cooler by the second. Now I was becoming a little afraid, more of the unknown than of anything else. After all I was only nine, what did I know about this *Christmas Wind* as I called Him except that He made the room feel wonderful and that I did not want to leave. I started to talk to Him. "Hi," I said, "I know that you are here. I really like the way you make everything feel so fresh and exciting like at Christmastime." As I began to speak to Him, the room became progressively cooler in response to my words until it became filled with joy and excitement. Now I knew that I was definitely not alone. I continued to walk around, to talk to God, and to ask Him about Himself. Somehow in my little mind and heart, I knew that this wind and joy in the library was God, but if you had asked me how I knew this, I could not tell you.

I was enjoying the experience so much that I almost forgot about the book I was asked to collect and of Sister Therese waiting for me under the covered way. I spent about twenty minutes talking to Him and asking Him all about Himself and who He was, but He would not answer me. I headed for the door, put my hand on the door handle, opened it, and was about to walk out the door when suddenly I remembered to collect the book for Sister. I had completely forgotten about it. What a reminder! The thought just flew through my mind at lightning speed! The quickness of the thought took me by surprise. Was this an answer to my question? I was surrounded by peace and joy. It was everywhere!

I turned around and headed over to Sister's chair to look for the book. It was easy to find. Things were just as she had said. It was the only one lying flat; all of the other books were on their sides on the shelf. I picked it up and looked at the front cover. It was a children's book of Bible stories. The front cover had a picture of Moses cowering away in fear at the sight of the burning bush. It got my attention, and I opened the book. It immediately opened to the page where Moses was talking to God in the form of the burning bush that was not being consumed by the flames. Immediately there was a cool wind blowing in the library again and more joy in the air. *How strange,* I thought. *Of all the stories in the book why should it open at this page?* It had so many other stories, Daniel in the lion's den, Noah and the ark and others. It had large print just for kids and beautiful illustrations. I began to read the story of how God appeared to Moses and spoke to him, sending him to Pharaoh in Egypt to set the enslaved Israelites free and to allow them to leave. I read and read, devouring the story as though it was food and I was famished. Miracle after miracle and plague after plague, I consumed the book and was captivated by the illustrations. Somehow the presence of the cool wind was making this story so very real to me as though I was actually there, caught up in the experiences which transpired in the Exodus story. Then came the glorious climax when God parted the huge Red Sea and the Israelites crossed over onto the other side traversing on the dry seabed, and the Egyptians gave chase into the parted sea that God closed back over them, drowning them. The illustrations were magnificent, and God had my undivided attention. *Wow! I did not know He could do such things. He is really all powerful,* I thought. *He could do anything!* However, what stayed with me more than the plagues that befell Egypt and the parting of the Red Sea was the burning bush experience where God appeared to Moses and they had a conversation. To me, this was far more exciting—a face to face encounter with God. I turned back the pages to where Moses met God in the burning bush and read it again eagerly, completely enthralled by it. As I did so, the cool wind began to circulate faster, and the atmosphere became progressively thicker with joy. The more I read the story of Moses beholding the burning bush, the more it became a very real experience to me. It was as though I was actually there with him cowering in fear before the bush, hearing God speak from within the inextinguishable flames, and experiencing with the same intensity—the awesome and petrifying Presence of God along with Moses. It was as though Moses' experience was happening in the library at the same time as I read the book. I could not shake the feeling or wake up out of the experience. *Was this really happening, or was it just a dream?* I remembered asking myself, totally captivated by what I could feel in the library while still in the midst of experiencing it. I remembered that Sister was still waiting for me under the covered way, but I was not ready to leave. What an experience. It would not leave my tender mind. It remained firmly planted within me. I reluctantly but quickly said goodbye to the cool Wind and walked out of the library, locking the door behind me.

I ran down the stairs and along the covered way, looking for Sister Therese to give her the book. She was chatting with a teacher when I found her, and I gave her the book and her keys. She thanked me for both and asked me if I liked the book. I replied without hesitating, "Oh yes, Sister, very much!" to which she promised that I could borrow it the next day because she was going to use it to teach a class today. There was that twinkle in her eye again, and she smiled as though she knew something. I could not shake the feeling that it was all a set up between God and her for which I was grateful. I thanked her and ran back to play with my friends; with my little heart full, yet wanting to enjoy more experiences like this one. I felt cool again as I ran away. It was Christmas all the time around her.

That whole experience left a lasting impression with me. I just could not forget it. The next day, Sister Therese taught on the same subject about how God appeared to Moses in the burning bush and spoke to him. I was dumbfounded! The experience of the day before was still freshly imprinted on my mind and went everywhere with me even in sleep, and now it was even on the lips of others. Out of all of the Bible stories in the book, Sister Therese chose to talk about this one. What were the chances of this? Was this all a coincidence? Needless to say, I listened carefully to what she had to say. Try as I may, I could not get the reality of the library experience out of my mind. It was a lesson that would change my life forever. At age nine, it was something that I decided I had to have in my life, and it soon became an all consuming fire within me. It was all I could think about.

That afternoon I went home and asked God to appear to me and to speak to me just like He did to Moses but nothing happened. I was very upset with Him. I cried to Him asking Him over and over again. Still nothing happened. I asked Jesus what made Moses so special that God would talk to him and show Himself to Moses. I pleaded and begged Him to appear to me, but He did not. I was devastated but even more than this—I was hurt, because I believed God loved me and would want to be with me especially since I wanted to be with Him. So for two weeks, I could not bring myself to serve Him on the altar at St. Dominic's Church. It took the full two weeks for me just to forgive Him for not appearing to me. This was no easy task. After all I was only nine years old, and I had resigned myself to accept that I was not as special as Moses and would never have God up close before my eyes like Moses did. Little did I know back then that God never forgets and that seventeen years later He would grant my request in ways that I could never have imagined possible.

A DATE WITH GOD

ONE SUNDAY MORNING while at New Life Christian Fellowship, (the church I now attended in Buckingham) I distinctly heard the Holy Ghost say to me that He wanted me to worship every night. There were no classes at night, so this worked out fine. But I did not realize until after a few days that what He really wanted to do was to lead me in worship to the Father and the Son every night. For nearly two weeks before He said this, I had been finding within myself an excitement and uncontrollable desire to worship that I did not put there. It just seemed to have been birthed inside of me by God. I had to appease it, or my heart felt like it would explode from the inside out. So one night in my room, I placed a CD into my stereo, turned up the volume, and sang along with it. In the beginning, this was the only way I knew how to worship, but the Holy Ghost refined the process, told me to insert a tape into my walkman, place the earphones into my ears, and to worship along with the tape. I had never done this before, but it turned out to be better than the stereo because the earphones kept out all of the external noises, making the worship more intimate.

The first night I worshiped, I followed the order of the songs on the tape. I knew nothing about divinely–led or Spirit–led worship. I was just a baby in Christ and had a lot to learn. So I did as the Holy Ghost instructed me and sang the first song along with the tape. Immediately, power fell! It fell like a hailstorm through the ceiling into my room, onto and into me. It felt wonderful and left me wanting more. I was instantly recharged, like a dead battery that had been suddenly jolted back to life by passing electricity through it. I had so much energy in my body that I thought I would explode, and I was so filled with joy that I could not get the smile off my face. I wanted more of this joy and power, so I worshiped along with the second song on the tape. Power fell again and this time with greater intensity. I sang the third song and then the fourth in this manner just simply following the order of the songs on the tape, and power fell continually until I was so strong I felt like I could move a mountain. With each outpouring of power came uncontrollable joy that gradually filled me, and by the end of the worship, I was so happy in the deep innermost recesses of my heart that nothing and no one could dampen the joy that completely filled me.

I was so happy and excited that I could not keep it to myself. I had to share it with someone, which I later learned was not always a good thing. (I learned to be selective about whom I hung out with after worship. Because if it was not the right person, they could drain me of the joy and power I had received, and I could not get it back until the next time I worshiped.) I really wanted to share it with someone, but it was now 1:30 a.m., and I did not want to wake anyone. So I tried to sleep but could not. The power that had entered my body and the energizing joy seemed to be coursing through the blood in my veins, and it made me so alive that it was difficult to sleep. I did not fall asleep for another hour.

The next morning I rose at around 7 a.m., fully charged and refreshed although I only had four and a half hours of sleep. It was all on account of the power that had fallen into my body the night before. It energized me supernaturally so that sleep was not necessary. I went through all of my university days like this, functioning on God's power and not on sleep. Each day I had sufficient energy to get me through it and even had a surplus of energy at the end of it. In fact the energy I received each night was always proportional to how much I would need the following day. From this I could tell how demanding the next day would be.

I worshiped like this for a few months to the kicking black gospel sounds of Jesse Dixon and Hezekiah Walker and then to the worship music of Ron Kenoly's *God Is Able* album. I loved that album and so did God. I worshiped to it every night for almost a year because the power on it would not leave and the songs dealt with God doing the impossible. This was on His mind and heart concerning my studies and upcoming exams.

Then the Lord led me to Ron Kenoly's *Lift Him Up* album, but something was missing. Something more fulfilling and even more satisfying than Jesus' power falling from the heavens, through the night sky and the ceiling of my dorm, into my body and heart to infill me with His love and power to live. Something or rather someone very precious was missing, and I did not know how to get Him in my life. I saw Him the morning after my baptism when He appeared to me in my bedroom and woke me with His awesome glory, Presence, and power filling my room. We talked (or rather He talked) for three hours, sitting on the edge of my bed. He appeared many times afterwards, but I did not know how to have His Presence at will when I needed Him or wanted to spend time with Him to get to know Him better. I did not know how to get Him every day of the week. He just showed up when He felt like, and I was left at His mercy. I did not know anything about Him at all. All I knew was that despite all of the power falling in my room—as beautiful as it was—I would never be complete until I had Him continuously in my life. He completed me, and I was ignorant of how to get Him. I did not just want power; I wanted His Presence.

Nobody taught about Him. I have heard many pastors in England teach about the gift of the Holy Ghost who comes into a born again person. He speaks, urges, nudges, and intercedes to the Father and the Son for us and so on. However, I have never heard anyone teach about the Holy Ghost who appears before me, speaks to me, performs wonderful miracles, and hugs me when I need a hug or who appears with such a thick and awesome presence, that the very skin on my bones would be singed off my body if He did not turn down His glory. Pastors in Barbados did not teach about Him either, and I was left at my wit's end. The Bible spoke about Him and this was what troubled me even more, because despite all of the accounts of the men in the Bible who walked hand in hand with God, saw His appearance, and dwelt where He dwelt, there was no pastor, evangelist, prophet, or teacher who taught about Him as an able–bodied person walking the face of the earth with men today. So I was left to solve my predicament of not having Him physically appear in my life, all by myself.

In Genesis He appeared to an aged Abraham to promise him that he would have a son in his old age. Abraham knew who was standing before him when God appeared to him. That was why he bowed down to the ground before Him calling Him Lord. This showed that

Abraham may have had previous dealings with God the Holy Ghost appearing to him in the past. In Genesis we are told that Adam walked with God hand in hand in the Garden of Eden in the cool of the evening. This means that he knew how God looked, how His hand felt in his own, and how His voice, and even how His laughter sounded. So did Enoch. Enoch walked with God, and God called him His best friend. How I envied Adam and Enoch to have experienced God the way they did. All these men were not talking about God the Father nor God the Son but about God the Holy Ghost. At the time He was the only part of the Trinity who lived on the earth until Jesus arrived of course.

In his youth Samuel slept in the temple, near to the dreaded but awesome Ark of the Covenant where the Manifest Presence of God sat on the mercy seat. (That was the seat created on the top of the box by the wings of the two cherubim. For God to sit on the mercy seat, He must have been in manifest form. He could not sit on it if He were in the form of a cloud or a pillar of fire.) He appeared to Moses first as a burning bush that remained unconsumed by fire. Then later on Mount Sinai, He spoke to and had fellowship with Moses for forty days at a time, who watched Him do amazing things like carve the law in stone with His finger. (More than likely, He used His index finger.) He also appeared to Elijah who knew Him well and knew His appearance. He also appeared to Shadrach,

Meshach, and Abednego in the fiery furnace to protect them from harm from the flames, but to top it off, King Nebuchadnezzar witnessed God the Holy Ghost walking around in the furnace with the three men he had put into the flames, when he said "Lo, I see four men loose, walking in the midst of the fire, and ... the form of the fourth is like the Son of God" (Daniel 3:24–25).

So why was no preacher in the world talking about Him and His appearing? I kept my eyes and ears open, but no one—no pastor, evangelist, bishop, or teacher—mentioned Him as a person whom one could be with and get to know. Even less, did they mention His appearance or His appearing before men? Yet the Old Testament says that the priest on the Day of Atonement (Yom Kippur) would tie a rope around his ankle and go past the holy place into the holy of holies. Here he would sprinkle blood upon the mercy seat on top of the Ark of the Covenant for the forgiveness of Israel's sins. So the priest knew what He looked like and knew of His appearing because he must have seen Him in the holy of holies, behind the veil when he went to do his duties. It was this same Manifest Presence of God who departed from His residence behind the veil when Jesus died on the cross, and who tore the veil in two from top to bottom from behind it, and Who was now free to appear to any of the believers and to walk with them and perform miracles for Paul and Peter.

David the psalmist knew about Him and that He lived on top of the Ark of the Covenant. That was why he wanted the Ark in his household but was too afraid to move it onto his own property. So he used Obed-edom the Gittite as a guinea pig to see what would happen to him, if he would perish or be blessed. Seeing that he was blessed, David moved the Ark onto his property (See 2 Samuel 6:12). However, ignoring this shortcoming of David, he was a man who wanted God as a physical reality in his day to day living. He wanted to be able to detect and relate to God with at least three of his senses (sight, hearing and touch), and he would stop at nothing until God granted this request. So he pleaded with God until He granted his wish. God Himself called David a man after His own heart, knowing fully well that he was a man after God—*period.* For this reason, God loved him. Furthermore, David did not want God to visit him from time to time; he wanted to take up permanent residence with God and live with Him as a physically real and tangible God—twenty four hours a day, seven days a week. Like two roommates who are the best of friends are around each other all of the time and share the same physical space every minute of every day, this is what David asked God for over and over until he got it. Just look at David's words,

> One thing have I desired of the Lord,
> That will I seek after;

> That I may dwell in the House of the Lord
> All the days of my life,
> To behold the beauty of the Lord
> And to inquire in His temple.
>
> Psalm 27:4

The first time I read this I knew nothing about the Scriptures, interpreting them with my mind instead of asking the Holy Ghost for the true meaning of the passages. The Holy Ghost had not begun to teach me the Scriptures yet, so I thought that "dwelling in the House of the Lord all the days of my life" meant that David was asking God to let him live in Heaven with Him for all eternity after he died. However, the Holy Ghost showed me that I was mistaken. Strangely enough this psalm is read at many funerals, but it has nothing to do with our eternal dwelling place. David asked to dwell in God's dwelling place *all the days of his life. All the days of his life* were lived on Earth while he was still alive not after he died when he entered and dwelt in Heaven. It was not a plea from David to live with God after he died. He wanted to live wherever God inhabited on the earth all the time. He wanted to live *behind the veil* with God's Manifest Presence everyday, every hour, and every minute that he had on the earth and was unwilling to settle for the visitation the high priest had on the Day of Atonement once a year. For David, every day must be Atonement Day. God heard David's request and granted it. This was the reason why God loved and blessed him so much because David's heart was set on wanting God's Manifest Presence in his life, and he persistently asked God for Him until he got Him. David wanted God Himself, *period.*

I was happy that David got God all to himself, but I was left with my predicament. I was lonely and needed my friend back, and it seemed there was no one around to tell me how to get Him back in my life. (The Bible does say how to get Him, but I did not know this at the time.) So I was left stranded and alone. I still worshiped every night at midnight, but His Manifest Presence was not with me. I did not ask God to help me or to explain how to get His presence. I just accepted it as my lot in life. However, looking back, I realize that His eye was on the sparrow and that He was watching me the whole time. He knew my plight and that I was looking for Him, so He proceeded to set me up to find Him.

• • •

I WENT HOME to thirteen South Ridge Christ Church Barbados for summer break, as I did twice during my studies because almost all of the students returned to their distant homelands, leaving the campus desolate and very lonely. I was there for maybe two days when one night I got a strong urge to go and chat with my mother in the computer room. I entered the room that was once my bedroom, sat down, and chatted with her while she worked on the computer. The room comprised mostly of shelves of medical textbooks and some non-medical books, a computer, printer, and a scanner. Then something (or as I now know) someone caused me to glance over to the dressing cabinet where my mother had a small collection of Christian books. My eyes just barely caught the title, *Good Morning Holy Spirit.* I was in the middle of conversing with my mother, and so I did not pay much attention to the title. I was actually in the process of walking out of the room when all of my insides and all of my body screamed out, *Pick up that book there is something in it for you!* I walked out of the room without picking up the book, and the further away I walked from the study—the stronger and more anxious the urge became to return to the study and take the book. It got to the point where I could not take it anymore; the persistence of whatever was inside of me to return for the book and read it was compulsively strong. Like a man who has left his wallet behind, is faced with an incessant and relentless nagging, that something crucial for his survival is being left behind and to return for it, so it was with the book. This compulsion to return for the book was not overwhelmingly strong so as to overpower me, I could still choose not to obey the urge; it was just that I did not want to. I wanted to obey. So I did not fight it anymore, I gave in, returned to the study and took the book off the dressing table. I looked at the cover of the book and noticed the title again. *Good Morning Holy Spirit.* The memory of how I had first met Him face to face in my bedroom the morning after my baptism, flooded into my mind and so was the awesome glory surrounding Him that morning. I read the back of the book where there was a brief synopsis of what or rather who the book was about, namely the Holy Spirit, and it described the writer, a man called Benny Hinn.

I read the name again smiling confidently to myself. I know who Benny Hinn is; I know him well. Isn't he that fairly tubby English comedian whose slapstick and sometimes perverse sense of humor had been popular for years in England. I was an avid fan. The man was very funny from his rosy cheeks to his wicked smile and his roly-poly figure, even his appearance was comical. *What is he doing writing a book on the Holy Ghost?* I thought. Very pleased with myself I asked my mother to borrow her book, which I took downstairs to my room, climbed into bed and began to read. Immediately the Spirit urged me to read the back of the book again. This time I realized the writer's name was *Benny Hinn,* not Benny Hill the comedian as I had previously thought. The latter is a jolly, pink, and chubby Englishman while the author of the book, from what I could gather was of Arab origin.

Just holding the book in my hand, I could feel that something was about to happen. The atmosphere in my room began to change. As I began to read, power fell through the ceiling into me, infilling me. What power there was on *Good Morning Holy Spirit!* There was the greatest touch of God's power on almost every page. I discovered that the areas of the book at which the power fell and at which I received an infilling of the Holy Ghost, were the areas that God wanted to bring to my attention and reflected what He wanted to say to me. The areas of the book that did not reflect what was on God's mind, which I did not need to take notice of, were not touched and had no power on them. They were just ordinary words. When reading the segments of the book that He wanted to bring to my attention, sometimes the power fell with such great force that all I could do was sit under His power raining down on me, infilling me unto overflowing. At the end of reading each day, I would put it down completely infilled and satisfied, totally empowered and energized by the Holy Ghost, with tear stained cheeks and so much power in my body, running through my veins, that I could not fall asleep for another hour.

I did not want to put it down, but I was forced to, having read it all day, all night and into the next morning. The only reason I stopped reading was because the sun was rising and I thought I should get some rest before the day began. I loved *Good Morning Holy Spirit* and so did God. He affirmed it over and over again, touching whole pages at a time.

I finished reading it in three days. It was a wonderful experience getting so close to God just by reading a book, and I thoroughly enjoyed it. Who would have thought that God would have met me through a Christian book other than the Bible? He never had before, nor has He done so since. But I realized the book answered all of my questions on how to get back my Holy Ghost and how to keep Him in my life. Furthermore, God Himself had sanctioned the book with so much power and approval, that it left no question in my mind, that He was responsible for this plot to restore me into His Manifest Presence once again.

By the time I completed the book, the pages were tear–stained, and I had such a wonderful time reading it that I was eager to read it all over again. However, time did not permit this as I had to return to university. Never mind, I now had the answer to my question on how to get the Holy Ghost in my life. In Luke 11:13 Jesus said, "If ye then, being evil, know how to give good things to your children, how much more shall your heavenly Father give the Holy Spirit to them that ask?" The Lord had shown me in *Good Morning Holy Spirit* that first one must ask the Father for the Spirit (Luke 11:13) and then second, invite the Holy Ghost over and over again to come into my presence until He eventually shows up. That was it! It was that simple! God had also used *Good Morning Holy Spirit* to show me that there was at least one man on the planet, to whom the Holy Ghost manifested Himself and fellowshipped with on a physically intimate level. I thank God that He did because I was beginning to think I was the only one (except for those men in the Bible who walked and fellowshipped with God's Manifest Presence and who had remarkable experiences with the Holy Ghost.)

Reading through *Good Morning Holy Spirit,* I realized that I had experienced almost all of Benny Hinn's encounters with the Holy Ghost almost one and a half years before reading Benny's book and this shocked me. They started when He first appeared to me just after my water baptism and continued for a year and a half (All with the exception of one when God gave Benny the vision of a man burning in eternal fire and telling him that if he did not preach the Gospel this would happen to others. I have never experienced this). Now I had company, even better, someone who was way ahead of me and was already in the ministry. All I needed to do now was to ask God the Father for the Holy Ghost and invite Him personally until He appeared in my day to day living experience, and once this happened, I could enjoy the same precious and intimate fellowship with Him that Benny Hinn enjoyed.

• • •

I GAVE THE book back to my mother and returned to England to resume classes, but the adventure was only just beginning. I immediately commenced worshiping at midnight every night, but this time I did what God had shown me in *Good Morning Holy Spirit.* I asked God the Father to send the Holy Ghost to me so that I could enjoy His friendship and fellowship, and

I spoke to the Holy Ghost directly, inviting Him to come into my reality and into my room to lead worship and to fellowship with me. In the beginning there was no one in the room just me and my walkman, but despite this I persisted (especially in the latter, which was especially difficult because with no one in the room other than myself, I felt very self-conscious addressing and conversing with someone who was not yet present) but speaking to Him as though He were. I felt like a child talking to his imaginary friend that only he could see, except in my case I could not see Him because He was not yet there.

After keeping the midnight date with God for about three to four weeks—all the while asking thc Father for the Holy Ghost and inviting the Holy Ghost to come to me—I began to see results. One midnight, I felt Him walk through my locked bedroom door and stand behind me while I was worshiping. I smiled as my room was instantly filled with joy, and I welcomed Him into my room and into my life. He kept His distance and stayed for the entire duration of my worship, touching one song after another as I sang along with my walkman. For the first few nights, He remained a little distance away, and as the nights went by, I coaxed Him and encouraged Him to come closer, which He did a little bit more every night. Sometimes I just talked to Him and He came closer of His own volition. In fact one night, He started talking after about one to two hours of worship, and He felt so comfortable that He approached little by little until He was just over one meter away. Altogether the whole process took about three weeks from the time He appeared up to the time He was sufficiently at ease around me to come right up to me.

On that fateful night when the Holy Ghost finally came right up to me, He stood in the doorway for a while. Then all of a sudden, there was a deep and intense hush, and He stood still. The whole room was filled with an air of the greatest expectation that something truly awesome was about to happen. Somehow I knew this, yet I did not know how. Then suddenly He broke the silence and began rendering the sweetest worship to Jesus, the Lamb on His Throne. His worship was gentle and soft and had an abundance of power on the song, "Lamb of God." All of me—my heart, my soul, my will—every part that was me and every cell that constituted me, raised its voice in adoration to the Lamb on His Throne who was slain for me. The Holy Ghost came closer to me and stood beside me. I could feel Him standing on my left hand side, and when He did this, the volume of the worship subsided. I felt a powerful force from above and behind me pushing me to the ground. I resisted at first, but then I allowed it to genuflect me onto the ground. I found myself kneeling on one knee with my head bowed low before the King of kings. Instantly the intensity of the power in the room rose to such an incredible height that all I could do was kneel and weep. I dared not stand. I couldn't. My heart was heavy with gratitude to the precious Lamb of God for what He had done for me at Calvary, and for the first time I was saying thanks and it seemed that He was responding to my saying thank you. Do not get me wrong, I had thanked Him many times in the past, but He never physically responded to my gratitude before and certainly not with such power. I felt that I was taken by the Holy Ghost into the Lamb's throne room to say thank you to Jesus in person and that He heard me and was saying, *You are welcome.* I waited still genuflected before the King in eager anticipation of what was to happen next. Then I got the urge to say it very softly, "Thank you precious Lamb of God. Thank you Jesus for Calvary." With that it started to rain power. Power began to fall from the ceiling like a hailstorm, like rainwater that burst an overhead tank that was being poured out endlessly and relentlessly with great force onto me. I stood up and basked in the power falling onto and into me, and I was infilled with the Spirit and recharged to overflowing.

Then the power stopped falling and the whole room began to be filled to full capacity with the extremely thick presence of the Manifest Presence of God. He was filling the room with Himself. There was so much of Him in my room that I dared not speak and I dared not move. I did nothing for fear of losing His precious presence. There was gradually more and more of Him, and when I thought no more of Him could fit into the room, He brought in even more of Himself. When He had ultimately saturated the room with Himself, I just stood there basking in His glorious Presence and enjoying every molecule of Him in my room. I stood there complete and in a state of blissful joy and indescribable happiness, weeping in the thickest presence of God I have ever experienced and thanking Him for coming right up to me and being with me that morning.

From that night onwards, my worship was never the same again. The presence of the Holy Ghost made a world of difference. Whereas before I worshiped from afar, now I worshiped from up close. Whereas before when I worshiped, I only had audio, now with the Manifest Presence of God in the room, I had surround sound and three–dimensional visual. As if that was not enough it was as though there were receptors on the Father's and Jesus' heart and mind so that through the Holy Ghost, I could tell what the Father and the Son were feeling and even thinking. I knew during the worship which words in the song "Lamb of God" were on Jesus' mind, and the Holy Ghost prompted me to sing those words over and over again until they were no longer what Jesus was trying to get across to me. Then He touched other words to show me other things that were on His mind. I could feel the emotion that was being stirred in Jesus' heart as that song was being sung to Him in gratitude for going to the cross in my stead as well as the intensity with which He felt them. His feelings were one of, *I did it willingly for you and would do it again for you if it were asked of me. I love you that much George.* Finally I could commune with the Father and the Son very intimately and very realistically. Such an intimate communion was only made possible by and through the Holy Ghost and this helped to explain to me a little more about how the Trinity worked—the three together as one. Now I knew what the Bible meant by,

> Howbeit when He, the Spirit of truth, is come ... for He shall not speak of Himself; but whatsoever He shall hear, that shall He speak: and He will show you things to come. He shall glorify me: for He shall receive of mine, and shall show it unto you. All things that the Father hath are mine: therefore said I, that He shall take of mine, and shall show it unto you.
>
> John 16:13–15

This means that it is the job of the Holy Ghost to relate everything that Jesus, and the Father says to us. He will not speak of His own accord and He will show us things which Jesus and the Father want us to see and to know. However, the function of the Holy Ghost even goes a step further. Jesus asked His Father, "[A]s Thou Father, art in Me and I in Thee, that they also may be one in us: that the world may believe that

Thou hast sent Me" (John 17:21). This brought me into even greater intimacy with the Father and the Son. The Holy Ghost inside of me could relay to me and let me experience the emotions and feelings that the Father or the Son were feeling at any given moment, so I could feel what they were feeling and share in their emotions as though we were one being. Their emotions are very strong, sometimes overpowering, and can linger for days at a time. Once, the Father was sad and I could feel His sadness coursing through my blood and my body almost overwhelming me. It went on day after day and night after night until I asked the Holy Ghost why I was so sad. He replied that it was the Father who was sad and not I and that I was just feeling His unhappiness. Then I asked the Holy Ghost what made the Father so sad, and He told me.

Now I understood what the Bible meant when it says, "Deep calleth unto deep" (Psalm 42:7). I believe that the Holy Ghost is the person who can reveal the deepest and most profound depths of the Father and the Son to the believer, and that it is impossible to access them any other way on the earth. I believe that this is what David the Psalmist was saying when he was talking about deep calling unto deep in Psalm 42:7. Here David was crying and thirsting for God and even hungering for the deeper things of Him that he had not yet experienced. If the Holy Ghost is the key to experiencing the utmost intimate depths of the Father and the Son, then all that is left for us to do—if we want to access these depths with each individual of the Trinity—is to ask the Father, Jesus, and of course the Holy Ghost to bring us into such close communion with the Holy Ghost Himself that we could access and be one with each member of the Trinity. Wouldn't that just be wonderful?

• • •

AS TIME WENT on, I began to notice a trait that I soon discovered was typically characteristic of Him. He was never late for one of our midnight worship sessions. Every night during the three week period, He was in my room at midnight sharp, never a second later. He was so punctual that you could set your clock by His appearing, and I soon did exactly that. Before He began appearing, I would keep an eye on the clock to see when it was midnight; at which time, I would put the books down and commence worship. Now there was no need for the clock because once He appeared and my room was filled with His glory, or once His Manifest Presence entered through the door and stood by my bedside, I knew it was midnight and time to commence worship. He was never late. Never. Once I asked Him why He was always so punctual, and my heart melted at His response, "I am punctual because I can't wait to be with you and worship with you. I don't want to waste the time I could be spending with you, being elsewhere. I look forward to the time we spend together every night. Those hours are the highlight of my day and are very precious to me."

A few nights later, I was late for worship. It was about quarter past midnight, and I was at a service being held by a man of God called John Barr in Buckingham town. He was a lovely man of God, whom I had the pleasure of meeting and getting to know for a little while after the service. Unfortunately, I was late for my date with God, and I knew that the Holy Ghost was anxiously waiting for me to come home and worship. I just knew He was there waiting. To this day, I don't know how I knew this. All I knew was that no matter how much I tried to ignore it, something in my veins and in my blood ["for the blood is the life" (Deuteronomy 12:23)] was telling me that He was in my room waiting for me to come home and worship. So I ran through the town in the cold night air and up the long hill towards the Verney Park Campus where I lived. I arrived at my dorm at about half past midnight and hurriedly inserted the key to unlock my door. I could feel there was an abundance of power on the other side of the door. I could feel it coming through the door. It felt like an overload of electric power. That is the best description I could give. However, I did not pay attention to it because I was concentrating on getting into my room.

As I flung open the door, I was floored. I was bowled clean over by a tidal wave of wind so powerful that it knocked me to the ground. I was in total shock at what had just happened. I sat on the ground looking up into my room, and there He was, standing near to the door that I had just opened, with His glory filling my room and His Presence everywhere, even encroaching into the hallway. Stunned, I slowly got to my feet and delicately approached the Holy Ghost who was smiling. What had happened was that He was so happy that I had come home to keep our date and to worship, that He greeted me with an enthusiastic hug at the door. However, His enthusiasm was so great that it was akin to being greeted by a mighty rushing wind with the potential to derail a freight train. I was in awe at what I had just experienced. It all happened so fast and so unexpectedly that I needed time to come to grips with the reality of God's tremendous power. The Holy Ghost was very happy that I had kept my date with Him. He melted my heart when He told me, "I love you George. I was missing you so much and when midnight came and went, I missed you even more. I kept calling you to come and worship with Me, and I knew that you would come. I knew that you would keep your date with Me." That night was the one–and–a–half–year anniversary since I started keeping the date with the Holy Ghost every midnight to worship, and the second night in that time since I had been late for worship. I have not been late since.

I never knew that God the Holy Ghost could fall in love with a man so completely and miss him when he is not with Him, and that He would express His love for the man so openly and admit that He missed him. That night deepened our relationship because from then onwards I knew that I was totally loved by God. I had read it in the Bible over and over many times, but that just does not compare to being told the words from His lips to my heart. I knew that I loved Him, but I never really knew how He felt about me until now. I was undone that God Almighty, the greatest and most powerful force in the universe, loved me and would choose to be with me. From that day onwards, I felt very special. Very special indeed, and even to this day, I cannot get over it. Now I knew what David meant when he called God the *Lover of his soul.* Now I understood why David gave God that title.

I responded to Him saying, "You are everything to me, and I love You with all my heart. I am so sorry that I was late for our meeting."

With that, the glory in the room began to thicken. He came closer to me and without saying a word just wrapped His arms around me and said, "It's okay." With His arms around me, I could feel His power coursing through my body from my head to my toes and back up again and my heart filling with joy even to a bursting point. He held me for a few glorious moments, and then He began to fill the room with His glory. He brought in more and more of Himself until the room was almost at bursting point. He continued to fill the room until there was no room left for anyone or anything else. There was so much of Him in the room now that I was afraid to speak lest I caused Him to leave. I did not know what behavior was acceptable in so much of His presence. I had never experienced so much of Him before, and no one ever taught me what to do in such a situation. So I decided to stay silent. Then just as I thought no more of Him could fit into the room, He brought in even more of Himself until He took over the entire room and occupied every atom of it. There was now so much of Him in the place, that the thick cloud of His presence distorted the light rays coming from the lights in the room, like a thick mist at dusk. At this point I no longer had the option of whether I should commence worshiping or stand quietly, as I was now physically unable to speak or sing. In fact I could barely stand in His presence. My knees kept buckling under my weight, and I slowly and quietly walked over to a wall on which I leaned for support. Eventually all of Him was in my room surrounding me with joy and awe, leaving me to lean in His utmost presence, weeping, unable to express my awe and my joy, unable to speak and barely able to stand. All I could do was weep and weep and weep in His awesome Presence. What a glorious moment!

There have been a few similar instances since this initial experience akin to (1 Kings 8:10–11) where the cloud of His presence entered the Temple that Solomon built for Him: "[A]nd the priests could not stand to minister because of the cloud, for the glory of the Lord had filled the house of the Lord . . . ," but none of them were as intimate or as overwhelming as this one. This remains the greatest gift God has ever given to mankind in the past and to me today—the awesome gift of Himself.

THE VISION OF THE THRONE ROOM OF THE KING:

The Angelic Worship

ONE NIGHT JUST before Christmas, I had my very first vision ever, and the sequence of events that followed was to puzzle me for many years to come until Jesus explained them to me. I was packing my suitcase to return home to Barbados for the Christmas holidays. My family always spent Christmas in Barbados, so although the three children were studying in England and Northern Ireland, we would always return home to spend Christmas with our parents. My father and mother disliked the cold and the snow and made it clear that they would not brave these elements at their age. Their rationale was that they traveled home from England and Ireland when they were university students to spend Christmas with their parents, and now it was their children's turn and duty to do so. Under no circumstances were they coming up to England to spend Christmas with any of us. So I was in the process of packing my suitcase, which I had not completed doing even by midnight and had to stop because I had a Visitor.

At twelve sharp, my room was filled with an air of expectancy and excitement, and ever so gently, the Holy Ghost walked in. It was twelve midnight, and it was time for our date. My whole room was quickly filled with a thick cloud of Him as He entered, and I was anxious to see what He was going to do tonight. I went over to Him and said, "Hi!" and wrapped my arms around Him and kissed Him. He then urged me to play a worship tape called *Lamb of God.* All of the songs on the tape worshiped and paid homage to Jesus the Lamb of God for buying us with His Blood and paying the price for our sins. That was the theme of the album. So I inserted the cassette into the walkman and began to sing the first song to Jesus, which was also called "Jesus, Lamb of God," and paid homage to Him seated on His throne. Then we began singing the second song, then the third, by that time my room was filled with the Holy Ghost to the point where it could not be filled any more.

The Angelic Worship

At that moment I had a vision. The very first vision God had ever given me. All of a sudden I was not in my room anymore. It was gone, and instead I found myself hiding behind an incredibly thick white pillar. Looking around, I realized it was one of hundreds of huge white columns that supported a very high ceiling to a grand white hall, with a total area of a little more than one hundred thousand square feet. It was huge. The ceiling was almost thirty to forty feet high, and everything was white and spotless.

The great hall was filled with what appeared to be hundreds of thousands of angels. They were all kneeling silently at first. Then they began to sing, then to chant in drone tones while bowing their heads to the ground, almost touching it. In perfect unison, they were worshiping a man seated on an absolutely huge throne made entirely of white precious stones. The man radiated a bright blinding white light so that I could only peer around the pillar enough to see the little toes of His left foot, before I felt the flesh on my face begin to burn. Whatever power was radiating from Him would have cooked my mortal body in seconds had I stepped out from behind the pillar. Also a totally white light radiated out of His body—the brightest, purest white light imaginable. It would have blinded me for life had I peered around the pillar to see more than what I had already seen. So for my own safety, I stayed just where I was, using the pillar for cover. I peered around it from time to time as far as I was able to see, trying to catch glimpses of what was going on. I was in awe at what I was seeing. I remember pinching myself to make sure that this was not a dream. The most I ever saw of the man on the throne were His feet. Then with all of the angels still on their knees and with their heads bowed reverently very close to the ground, they proclaimed in perfect unity one with another to the man on the throne, "Worthy are You Oh Lamb to receive glory and honor and power!" It was then that I saw seven fires burning just below the feet of the Lamb on the Throne. They were the closest things to Him. The fires were in tall narrow golden lamp stands.

At that moment the Holy Ghost appeared just next to me behind the pillar. I was pleased to see Him because I was in unfamiliar territory here and needed His presence to guide me through it. He told me that the seven fires are the seven Spirits of the Holy Ghost. They are called Wisdom, (which Solomon had), Knowledge, (as in Word of Knowledge), Power and Might, (which Samson had) to name a few. Behind the lamp stands were about twenty or so men who also joined the angels worshiping the Lamb on the Throne. However, they were not angels; they were humans and were standing at the foot of the throne between the lamp stands and the troops of angels. They were closer to the Lamb on the Throne than the angels were, and wore golden crowns on their heads that looked very heavy, as if they were made of solid gold. They wore very rich white robes, and they also bowed low before the Lamb on the Throne in unison with the angels. Then in an instant, the singing and chanting ceased, and in perfect unison all of the angels stood upright with their heads still slightly bowed. It was then that I saw the size of these magnificent beings and their unsurpassed beauty. The Holy Ghost said, "Their number is ten thousand times ten thousand and thousands of thousands." There was a sea of them—a truly awesome sight to behold! They all averaged about seven feet tall measured with their wings folded, from the tip of their massive wings over their heads to the base of their heels where the wings ended. Their wings had large white feathers, and their bodies glowed with a bright white light. They were beautiful.

What got my attention was that they were all male. There were no females. They were all backing me, so I could not see what they looked like from the front. But from what I could see, they were nothing like what books and drawings had led me to believe. They were far more beautiful and far more impressive than any artist's impression I had ever seen. They were all strong muscular beings; some carried long golden swords while others held long golden bows, wearing quivers on their shoulders laden with long arrows. They were regimented and ordered and powerful; what a beautiful sight!

I felt very safe knowing they were on my side. The troops of angels were built solid and had an air of imperviousness and invincibility. Their posture was ramrod straight, and they were very strong creatures. Most of them were warriors. Each angel towered seven feet in the air with the exception of seven of them who were about half a foot taller than the others. The Holy Ghost called the taller ones, archangels, or chief angels. They were the seven highest angels in the hierarchy of the angelic host. The Holy Ghost pointed out the most powerful looking one who wore a huge golden sword and scabbard about his waist and said, "He is Michael the commander of the armies of the Lord and God's strategic advisor, who remained faithful to God during Lucifer's rebellion, and with His armies waged war against Lucifer and threw him and his followers out of Heaven." Then the Holy Ghost pointed out another tall and muscular archangel, this one He called Gabriel and yet another He called Pravuil, who is the wisest of all the angels and the fastest thinking angel in Heaven. The Holy Ghost also pointed out Raphael and three others, but they were too far away for me to have a good look at them. All of the angels came to their feet in one unified swift movement. None were early and none were late; they were perfectly unified by some invisible force that orchestrated and ordered the worship. Suddenly, they burst into the most glorious sound of worship I had ever heard. It was not of the earth.

Very high pitched sounds emanated from their mouths, and although my ears could barely withstand such high frequency sounds, I wanted to hear it all. The worship was no longer angels singing to the person seated on the throne; it had surpassed that to all different languages. (It wasn't English, French, or any earthly language but something sounding as though it was from another planet and comprising of high pitched notes.) Yet although the angels now sang in different languages in different melodies and with different rhythms, the music and the worship were always in time, never out of synchronization and perfectly orchestrated, so that every note and word meshed together perfectly. It was the most beautiful worship I have ever heard and probably will ever hear in my lifetime before returning home to Heaven. So far there is nothing on the earth like it.

I was enjoying this grand affair and taking it all in when the angels all bowed down before the Lamb on the Throne again, continuing their singing to Him as they did this, and then they stood up again, still singing the whole time. I noticed how happy and joyous the angels were as they worshiped the Lamb on the Throne. Now they began to worship the Lamb of God singing in English, and to my surprise, they were singing the exact same songs that we were singing at Christian Union and at church every Sunday for the past three weeks. Song after song, they were singing the very songs we were using to usher God's presence into our services. Just then I realized that both men on

Earth and the angels in Heaven were singing the same songs to worship the King on His throne in the same season. This was no coincidence, and the Holy Ghost would explain all about this to me a few weeks later. In the very last row of angels just in front of my pillar, one of the angels turned around and looked right at me. I hid behind the pillar hoping he had not seen me. I was afraid he would sound the alarm if he spotted me; because aside from the twenty or so men in the front row, I was the only human there, and I did not know if I was allowed to witness these things. I peeped around the pillar once more, and he was looking right at me with a smile on his face and my fear of being reported dissipated. He then winked his left eye at me, turned around, and resumed worshiping the Lamb on the Throne. Immediately the Holy Ghost, who was standing to my left hand side and left of the pillar, said to me, "He is your guardian angel." I could not believe what I was hearing. I had grown–up thinking that guardian angels were only found in children's stories. I had not read a lot of the Bible as yet, so I did not know if this was so or not.

So I asked the Holy Ghost, "What is his name?" He knew I doubted Him.

I could feel it in His response to me when He said, "His name is Seth." When the Holy Ghost mentioned his name to me, Seth heard, turned around, and smiled at me once again, then turned back around to resume worshiping the Lamb on the Throne.

• • •

WITH THAT THE vision ended just as suddenly as it began. I was once again in my dorm room, and the Holy Ghost was still by my side. I could not believe what I had just seen. I had to sit down just to digest what I had just experienced. It was overwhelming. I asked the Father for proof immediately just to convince my mind that I was not going mad. I asked Him that if what I had just witnessed was real then He was to give me visible, audible, and tangible proof within the next couple of days.

Meanwhile, the Holy Ghost urged me to resume worship for about twenty minutes more, after which I completed packing my suitcase. It was now early Friday morning, my flight would be in a few hours, and I was anxious to return to my island home.

AN ANGEL IN THE CANE FIELD

THE FLIGHT HOME was uneventful except for the fact that I was not permitted to smoke on the plane. It was very uncomfortable enduring an eight hour flight from England to Barbados without a cigarette. After about five hours, I started to experience nicotine withdrawal, and the high altitudes made the withdrawal pangs even worse. I had been saved the previous year (a few days before Christmas 1996), and I came to God an occasional drinker and a habitual smoker. Initially beer was my drink of choice at parties, but sometimes I enjoyed the odd glass of sherry or what was slowly becoming my favorite, a glass of red wine, preferably a Chianti. Three months after my salvation experience,

God took the alcohol out of my system in a very dramatic and powerful way, and I lost all desire to drink. However, up to the time of the vision of the throne room, He did not ask me to surrender the cigarettes. This was good because every time I tried to quit smoking in my own strength—of which there were many, thinking it would please God—I never succeeded. I simply could not do it. Each time was a very painful experience, too painful to do on my own. It had a very strong hold on me, and I leaned on it to deal with the pressures of life and to cover emotional wounds from the past. I had been a smoker for over twelve years and smoked an average of twelve cigarettes per day everyday. During exam time this number increased to about twenty cigarettes per day.

• • •

BEING BACK HOME in Barbados was always a treat. I always missed home, my parents, our house, and my country itself where I have lots of friends and almost everyone knows one another. It is an island of only one hundred and sixty-six square miles with a population of approximately two hundred and seventy-nine thousand people. I arrived home on a weekend and planned to attend the weekly men's fellowship meeting on Monday. Once I was home, I attended it weekly. The group consisted of about seven men who met to talk about things that affected them or were peculiar to men, and to pray or to simply hang out together. It comprised of a fairly tightly knit group of men who were good friends. The meeting was held every Monday at one of the elder's offices in a place called Rockley. The building was located just opposite one of the most popular beaches on the island called Accra Beach. It is along the popular south coast of the island where most of the young locals and visitors go to swim, tan, surf, boogie board, jet ski, shop, lunch, brunch, dine, or just simply relax. The coast is lined with very good restaurants and hotels on the beach side, not to mention the oodles of shops and malls with duty free shopping along the way. One could spend a full day there because there is so much to do.

On this particular Monday, my car was being serviced at the garage. It was such a nice day that I decided to walk to the south coast and take one of the many mini buses that frequently ran up and down the coast road past the office. I gave myself ample time to get there for the 4:00 p.m. meeting (almost a whole hour extra), so I left my parents' house on foot at about 2:00 p.m., heading due south taking shortcuts through various sugar cane fields. Growing up in Barbados, I learned some of the trails that ran through the cane fields in my area. They always proved to be useful when making journeys on foot or on bicycle because I could avoid walking along the much longer main roads and get to my destination much quicker. Sugar is one of the main export products of Barbados, and the fields in which the sugar cane is grown (from which sugar is extracted and exported) meander throughout the countryside of the island. Locals enjoy going for a stroll through them from time to time especially after the cane has been harvested, leaving large empty open fields. I prefer walking through them when the cane has not yet been harvested. However, roaming through narrow trails that are flanked on each side by hundreds of furrows of seven to eight foot sugar cane plants is not the safest place to be. There is always the fear of being mugged while walking through an unharvested cane field. It was now three days after my vision, and I had my Bible in one hand, my cigarettes in the other, and some change for the bus in my pocket. I had resigned to ask my Father for help in the area of quitting smoking because I found it too difficult and too painful to quit on my own. Needless to say, I was very disappointed with myself being a Christian and smoking at the same time.

I walked through the cane field behind my parents' house into the back of a residential area that I continued through until I got to the main road. I walked down a long gentle hill until I came to a highway that overlooked the south coast road. I then took a shortcut through a nearby cane field to get to the coast road instead of following the highway, because the former route was much shorter. I headed into the cane field following a well traversed path, which went down into a small valley that then went up a fairly steep hill before the terrain leveled off at the top of the hill. Some parts of the sugar cane were harvested, but most of it towered above my head, averaging about seven feet in height. Sugar cane arrows sprouted from the top of the plant, signaling that the cane was ripe and ready to be harvested. I climbed up the semi-steep hill following the trail, walking among the very tall sugar cane and enjoying the warm wind blowing through the field.

When I arrived at the top of the hill, I could hear reeds rustling, and two men were approaching me going in the opposite direction along the same path. As I walked past them, I observed them. They walked in single file, a short pudgy character in front and a tall, slender, sleek but muscular individual behind. They were both of dark complexions. The short one in front carried a cutlass with him, and they were both wearing dirty jeans and dressed like cane field workers who tended to the crop. The shorter one wore a hat to shade his face from the sun, and they walked fairly quickly as if they were heading home after a long day's work. As I passed them, I politely said good evening and continued on my way, not making eye contact with either of them. Part of me was a little afraid as I remembered stories of people being mugged in cane fields, and here I was alone in a cane field with two strangers—

and one of them had a cutlass. I watched them walk past me through the corners of my eyes and monitored their progress behind me, waiting for them to disappear down the hill. Suddenly, the tall man stopped in his tracks and turned around to face me. Immediately, I quickened my pace, my heart began to race, and I began to think of what I should do if this man were to attack or mug me. *I did not have that much money on me,* I thought, and I clenched my Bible and cigarettes very tightly, ready to run at a moments notice. That was my only recourse. I was going to run. The taller man was about six meters behind me when he turned around to face me. I thought to myself that this was enough of a head start if I had to out run him. Thc short man in front just kept on walking down the hill and soon disappeared from view.

"Could I have a cigarette?" the tall man asked politely, but I was wary that this may just be a ploy to bridge the six meter gap between us.

"Yes. Sure." I replied and warily flipped open my packet of cigarettes, removed one and held it out to the man, cautiously approaching him as he approached me. I did not look at his face. I was too afraid to do so. I just focused on running away from him at a moment's notice.

He took the cigarette from me and politely said, "Thank you."

"You are welcome," I replied as I turned and walked

away, but he still stood there and remarked with surprise in his voice,

"Wait a minute! You have cigarettes in one hand and a Bible in the other?" he asked genuinely. Well all fear turned to mortal embarrassment at that moment. I wished the earth would just open up and swallow me whole. I felt so ashamed that I could not raise my head to look at the man or to reply to him.

I did not know what to say but the truth, "God is still working." I answered sheepishly, as I continued walking away from him.

His voice echoed through my ears and my spirit when he said, "Do what He says, and He will bless you."

I heard what he said, waved, and replied, "Okay I will" and continued walking away, not paying attention to the words he had spoken. He stood his ground and firmly reinforced his message.

"Did you hear what I said?" he shouted after me. There was something about how he said this and the next statement that caused me to want to turn around. "Do what He says and He will bless you." He repeated firmly and loudly. I could feel his eyes piercing into my back. Something about these words got my attention and immediately tremendous power fell from Heaven onto me. Now he had my undivided attention. I realized that this man was showing me something that had a hidden truth inside of it, but I did not know what it was. All I knew was that at that moment, God had affirmed His message to me. I turned around to find out more about what he was saying and what he meant by this statement, and for the first time, I looked up to his face and into his eyes. His eyes were not human. They were glassy and strong, piercing yet loving. He smiled at me. Then it hit me. I stood there motionless, shocked at whom I was meeting face to face. It was Seth, my guardian angel, whom I had seen in the vision three nights earlier. I was in shock. I knew him by his seven foot tall slender yet muscular body, with his gentle smile and fiery eyes. He smiled at me when he realized that I had finally recognized him and knew who he was, and he winked his left eye at me just as he had done three nights before in the throne room of the King. I stood there dumbfounded with my legs quivering below me. I did not know whether to run to him and ask the multitude of questions that I had at that moment and from three nights before, or if to resume my journey to the men's fellowship. I did not know what to do. I had never seen an angel before in real life. I noticed he had no wings.

He smiled continuously and repeated one last time not as loudly this time but reassuringly, "Did you hear what I said?" He did not wait for an answer but again said, "Do what He says, and He will bless you." Power fell on me again from above.

"I will!" I promised after him, smiling at him. I was paralyzed. I wanted to run to him, talk to him, and see him up close, but my legs refused to move. I just stood there smiling at him and wanting to say so much and to ask him even more, but my mouth was glued shut. I smiled apologetically at him, and he in turn smiled back, turned, and walked away from me, heading down the hill into the valley. Within seconds he was out of view. I did not know what to do. A big part of me wanted to chase after Seth and ask him the questions that were racing through my mind at that moment, while another part of me was still in shock and tried to digest, remember, and analyze our meeting. Another part of me wanted to resume my journey to the men's fellowship meeting because time was ticking away. I stood there for a while trying to figure it all out. Then I tucked my Bible under my arm and sprinted towards the hill after Seth. I decided this experience was far more important than a men's fellowship meeting. I ran carefully down the hill, and not seeing anyone I continued into the valley, all the time looking into the furrows and rows of sugar cane plants for Seth, but there was no sign of him. I looked into the fields to my left and my right. No sign of Seth. I kept running until I caught up with the short man with the cutlass. I stopped, tapped him on the back, and wheezed at him—thanks to those confounded cigarettes.

"Excuse me." I gasped for breath, "Excuse me sir." He turned around. "Sorry to bother you, but where is your friend?" He asked me to repeat the question. He could not make out what I was saying from all of my wheezing. "Where is your tall friend, who was walking behind you when you passed me at the top of the hill?" He looked at me like I was certifiable, as though I was smoking something other than cigarettes.

"What do you mean? There was no one walking with me when I passed you earlier on," he replied. I froze.

"Are you sure?" I implored even more, bombarding him with even more questions, knowing that he was fed up answering them and now I was even insulting his intelligence.

"I would know if someone was walking behind me, wouldn't I?" He responded nastily, obviously offended. I tried to apologize, but it was too late. He already took offense at my question and resumed walking away from me. I apologized for wasting his time. He ignored me. I decided to let things be. Was Seth hiding in one of the furrows, had he just disappeared, or had he flown up towards Heaven? I had more questions than ever before. I walked slowly back to the hill checking in every furrow, looking to the left and to the right for any sign of Seth, but I could not find him anywhere. I climbed the hill again, and still there was no sign of him. I resigned to let things be, kicking myself for not going after Seth sooner or accosting him when I had the chance, when we were in conversation. I resumed my journey to the men's fellowship meeting. I came out at the other end of the cane field, walked for a few minutes down the highway, and caught a bus that was traveling along the south coast road. It dropped me just outside the elder's office in Rockley, and I went inside.

The men's fellowship usually lasts for two hours from four o'clock to six o'clock in the evening, but today it would last for nearly three. As I sat in the meeting, listening to the pastor and a few of the elders share their experiences of the past week, one single message seemed to be coming across, that they were blessed if they did what God told them to do. Imagine my excitement when I told them that about half an hour before, I had met my guardian angel in a cane field, and he told me the same words and message that was coming across now in this very meeting. My jaw dropped as I saw what was either the biggest coincidence in my life, or God was trying to get my attention with this message. I told them everything about the vision of Jesus in His throne room, the regiments of worshiping angels, seeing Seth among the back row of angels, and meeting Seth face to face in the cane field. They must have thought I was crazy, but the fact remained that the angel had taught me the message before I was to hear it from the lips of men, even my pastor. I knew it was no coincidence that the message spoken by the angel was the same as the one being heard now, but why? Was there something hidden in the message that I did not realize or understand at the time? It seemed fairly straightforward to me. I did not give it any more thought that day; however for the next six weeks, everywhere I went, all

I heard preached and taught was the same message, *Do what God says and He will bless you.* I heard it preached three Saturdays in a row at my Bible study in Barbados, two consecutive weeks by two different preachers at the People's Cathedral (a church I attended on Sundays in Barbados), a few times on the radio, and for three consecutive weeks in my Wednesday night cell group meetings held by The Living Room Church. Even when I returned to the University of Buckingham it was preached at New Life Christian Fellowship Church for three consecutive weeks, and also at the Christian Union meetings on Wednesday evenings for two weeks.

Whenever I came across all these different people teaching this message, I never informed them of this ongoing phenomenon of the message following me for six weeks even as far as England. Instead, I just listened to what they had to say concerning the message. Every time I heard them teaching this message power fell from Heaven into me, infilling me and marking the Father's affirmation of the message. This happened the first time I heard the message from Seth's mouth, and every time I heard it since then. One time while receiving an infilling of the Holy Ghost when I heard this message taught, the Holy Ghost informed me that there is more to the message than meets the eye. Something was hidden in the message. As to what it was, it would be seven years from my salvation date before He would reveal the hidden meaning behind it, which he did just in time to save my life both earthly and eternally; however, that is another story for another time.

After I left the men's fellowship that day and returned to my parents' house, I asked the Holy Ghost what Seth's appearance in the cane field was all about? He replied that after the vision of the throne room I had asked the Father for proof that the vision was true and real, and if it was actually what the angelic worship of the Lamb of God was like. So He sent Seth down to the cane field to cross paths with me so that I could meet him in the flesh, and I would not doubt the vision that I had seen. The truth is I had forgotten that I had asked the Father for proof of the authenticity of the vision. So the Father was doing what I had asked Him for and there I was asking Him why. Today there is no doubt or question in my mind as to the vision of the Lamb's throne room, of the angelic worship, and of meeting Seth my guardian angel.

BENNY HINN

MY MOTHER WAS visiting my youngest sister Lecia in Leeds and keeping her company as she was about to take a very difficult set of exams. Mom had gone to Leeds to give moral support at a time when Lecia needed it most, and to this end my mother rented a beautiful two bedroom house that she moved into for the duration of Lecia's preparation for her exams. Lecia lived with two flat mates, who were also students at the University of Leeds, in a flat very close to the campus, but Lecia soon moved in with Mom to study in quieter and more peaceful surroundings until her exams were over.

I had a two week vacation coming up, so Mom called to invite me up to Leeds to spend it with Lecia and her. Deep down inside, I was very excited about the whole trip although I did not really know why. There was just an inexplicable excitement in my bones and deep down in my soul.

Little did I know back then that God was setting me up, and that I was walking right into a plan of His that He had concocted and hidden far up His sleeves. When my two week holiday arrived, I took a coach from Milton Keynes to Leeds and sat in the back to enjoy the two to three hour journey and the gorgeous scenery of the lush English countryside. All of a sudden, my eyes caught a glimpse of a name, *Benny Hinn,* on the cover of a book being read by a young man in his late teens seated three seats ahead of me. I was immediately intrigued. What is it about this man? Is God trying to get a message across to me about Benny Hinn? At the time, I did not take any notice of God's subtle way of pointing me gently but persistently in this direction. So I just wondered to myself as to what was going on and sat back to enjoy the drive. Suddenly out of the corner of my right eye, just like before, I caught a glimpse of his name again, *Benny Hinn.* Now I sat up (God had my full attention), unable to believe my eyes because now there was an older gentleman sitting way up in the front of the bus, to the right of the aisle, reading another book by Benny Hinn. Was this coincidence or providence?

I now sat on the edge of my seat that was the very last seat in the back of the bus, situated smack in the middle of the aisle, so I could see everything going on in the bus ahead of me. Up to this point, I had not realized what God was up to, but I did notice that the two men were reading different books; one was grayish in color and the other cream. I sat there pondering what was going on when once again I sat back to enjoy the ride, until little by little, one by one, a few more people in the bus began to bring out books and novels to read along the journey. I watched as they opened their books to dog-eared and bookmarked pages and began to read. To my surprise, each cover had the same name on it—*Benny Hinn, Benny Hinn, Benny Hinn*... This was just too much now! I sat up and scrutinized the bus occupants; there were so many people reading his books that it made me wonder if I were on a bus to a Benny Hinn convention. I looked around some more and realized that yes there were a lot of people reading Benny's books but not everyone. There were some people reading newspapers and books by other authors, but this was still uncanny and unbelievable. *Was there a sale on Benny Hinn's books back in Milton Keynes which I did not know about, or did Leeds have a lot more Christians than the rest of England?* I pondered these questions for a little while before I resigned myself to relax and accept the fact that I did not know the answers to my questions. What I did know was that there were a lot of Benny Hinn's books being read in this one bus, and the readers' attention seemed to be avidly captured almost uninterruptedly by the author. Whatever or whoever held the reader's attention so intensely? I pondered this all the way to Leeds city.

Mom met me at the coach station in Leeds. She had rented a car for the duration of her stay, and so she collected me and took me to the house. It was in a quiet, posh residential area that was not too far from the happenings in Leeds city center, but not close enough to hear the traffic and the noise. The houses in the area were beautifully designed, and some had carefully manicured lawns. Mom's house was no different. It was all white and had high ceilings and doors with large windows. The inside was kept toasty warm by a roaring fire that did wonders to dispel the cold of the March evenings, along with hot toddy or hot chocolate that I soon realized had become a little evening tradition for Lecia and Mom. Needless to say, it soon became mine also. The house was a large one bedroom house, and so Mom and Lecia shared a bed while I slept in a huge pull–out bed in the living room sofa. I loved its firmness and size. It was very comfortable. The only set back was that the living room was my bedroom and that meant that I had a television in my bedroom.

Lecia seemed quite relaxed for someone with big exams only a few weeks away. This meant that Mom and I were doing our job well because the purpose of the whole exercise was to offer her support throughout her exams and keep her calm.

Later that night, I was nursing a mug of hot chocolate and reading one of my textbooks. When I got fed up of what I was reading and wanted to read something else, I strolled over to the dining table where Mom had a few books, medical journals, and her Bible. I perused through them and was shocked at what I found. There in the midst of the books was *Good Morning Holy Spirit.* My eyes bulged out of their sockets, and all the hairs on the back of my neck stood up on edge. I was very surprised to find that my Mother had brought it from Barbados with her. I held it lovingly, almost with disbelief at the fact that it was here. I asked Mom if I could borrow it, and she said yes. With that I immediately sat down at the dining room table that was in the living room just behind the sofa and the television and turned to page one. There was no separate dining room, and my Mother and Lecia were sitting in the living room reading and studying respectively.

Within seconds the Holy Ghost appeared at the dining room table, standing right next to me. I had not even reached page three yet, and there He was. Instantly the whole living room was filled with His glory, with a thick mist of joy slowly circulating in the air, and its atmosphere was charged with electricity. I closed my eyes and savored every morsel of Him. Not wanting to waste any precious moment of such awesome glory by speaking or doing something silly because He is far too precious to waste. I enjoyed all that I could drink up of His glory before I opened my eyes and looked over at Him.

"Hi," I whispered softly so that the others could not hear me. "How are you my Friend?" I asked.

"Fine thank you," He replied.

"Are you going to spend my holiday with me?" I implored.

"Yes," He replied.

"Will you be with me this time around as I read this book again?" I asked. He gave no oral reply but just turned His glory up a notch and smiled. Wow! What wonderful glory! Were it any stronger it felt like my skin would have been scorched and would have fallen off my bones. I continued to read *Good Morning Holy Spirit,* and His presence grew greater and greater in intensity so that I could not help but weep heavily. My tears dripped onto the already tear–stained pages of the book. I tried to hold them back, but His presence was so strong and thick that I had no choice but to let the tears flow. It was like a little rivulet at the beginning, but as I continued to read the book, His presence became even more intense; and I cried even more. It could not be helped. Everything that the Lord touched in the book (and there was at least something on every page) hit me with power from above, and was accompanied with infilling of the Holy Ghost and with weeping, because of His ever-increasing presence. His presence grew thicker and more intense every time I read something that was on His mind that He wanted me to notice in the book, and there were many things.

This second reading of *Good Morning Holy Spirit* was a totally different experience from the first time I read the book; because the first time I read it, it was to find out how to get the Holy Ghost manifest in my life. He manifested Himself in my bedroom for a few months after my baptism, but I did not know how to get Him back at will. This initial reading of the book was accompanied by lots of power falling through the ceiling into me, energizing me and infilling me with the Holy Ghost, but there was no presence. There was power but no presence.

The book explained how to get the presence of the Holy Ghost in my life from Luke 11:5–13, by asking the Father for Him and inviting the Holy Ghost to come and fellowship with me. I did this for a few weeks until one Sunday morning at Church, the Holy Ghost asked me to start worshiping every night at midnight, and from then onwards He appeared to me every night at this time. Now I was reading *Good Morning Holy Spirit* for the second time, but this time—in contrast to the first time—I had the person of the Holy Ghost manifestly present standing right beside me as I read every page. I had found Who I had set out to find and was enjoying every minute I spent with Him. I thought how funny it was that God had orchestrated the first reading of *Good Morning Holy Spirit,* and now here He was doing the very same thing with the second reading. I wondered why He wanted me to read the book a second time, and I waited eagerly for Him to tell me. I would soon know.

The more I read, the more the Holy Ghost began to remind me of the events that I had experienced that were very similar to what Benny Hinn had experienced and shared in his book. I could not believe that there were things that both he and I had experienced.

The first similarity was the way we were both energized after worship. After four or five hours of worship in my midnight dates with God every night, my body was exhausted and begged for rest, but my mind and spirit were charged with energy. So when I lay down to catch a few hours of rest before the sun rose, there would be intermittent surges of electricity running up and down my body. I would lie there wide awake with my eyes open for at least an hour or two, because I was completely recharged within but completely discharged on the exterior. My body could not keep up with my mind and spirit, and so I had to allow it to rest. Benny Hinn had a similar situation. After eight to ten hours of worship and fellowship with the Holy Ghost, his body was weary to the bone, but his spirit was still stirring. There would be intermittent surges of power running up and down his body during the night.

Unlike Benny Hinn however, I met the Manifest Presence of the Holy Ghost for the first time in my bedroom the morning after my baptism. The only person who I had ever heard of meeting Him was Moses. I did not know of anyone else at the time. I did not know many Bible characters. I was a young Christian and had a lot to learn. Benny Hinn met the Person of the Holy Ghost after attending his first Kathryn Kuhlman service.

Another similarity was that bedrooms seem to be the meeting place of choice for the Holy Ghost. Benny Hinn spent countless hours, months, and years fellowshipping, worshiping, and praying with the Holy Ghost in his bedroom. I too spent all of my time with the Holy Ghost there. It was where we first met and where we continued to meet every midnight for years to come—worshiping, fellowshipping, reading the Bible, talking, and basically just hanging out together. Each time the Holy Ghost would appear in my bedroom, my body would begin to vibrate and shake as God's presence increased until He completely filled my room. Benny Hinn described the same vibrating of his bones and shaking of his body whenever God's presence was very concentrated or very strong.

I was in awe when I read that the great evangelist Kathryn Kuhlman said that the Holy Ghost was more real than anything in this world. It was as though she was expressing the opinion of my heart, because to me He is my closest and dearest Friend. My Soul Mate. My Everything. Nothing and no one in this world can compare to Him.

As I continued to read, the similarities persisted. When I am in His Presence in my bedroom and I speak to Him, the atmosphere of glory and the ever thickening mist of His glorious Presence increases, usually with electricity in the atmosphere. Throughout *Good Morning Holy Spirit,* Benny Hinn constantly described the glorious atmosphere that filled his room whenever the Holy Ghost visited him there.

Another similarity was that Benny Hinn received a fresh daily infilling every time he spent time in prayer. This was something very personal to me too. When I was ill and suffering from depression, I relied on Prozac to get me out of bed every morning and to get me through the day. Before I became ill, I relied on coffee every morning to fuel me throughout the day. However, after I was healed Jesus made it abundantly clear to me that the infilling of the Holy Ghost that I received every morning was all the energy that I would ever need to live the day. So every morning before heading off to class, I received a daily infilling to empower me to live the day to the fullest. The Holy Ghost would come and breathe (His breath) into me in quick short bursts through my nose and mouth, similar to a resuscitation. I would never have got through a day without it. I still cannot.

Another similarity was that the Holy Ghost was in the habit of coming over and sitting on my bed beside me. He would appear in my room, we would talk, and then before I knew it He would make His way over to my bed and have a seat. He was very comfortable around me. I always knew where He was because His location was the source from which His intense glory emanated. Like a bush on fire in a room—if you have your eyes closed and just rely on your sense of touch—you can tell where the fire is coming from. So it is also with determining the Holy Ghost's location where He is standing or sitting in the room.

Further similarities include that my grandfather, George Hanoman, gave me and presented me to God soon after I was born, and Benny Hinn's mother gave him to God in return for God fulfilling her request for a son. Benny Hinn was named after Benedictus, patriarch of Jerusalem, the man who christened him in the Greek Orthodox Church, and I was named after my grandfather George, the man who presented me to God.

Another similarity was that both Benny Hinn and I went to Catholic preschools and primary schools. He was formally trained by nuns and later by monks for fourteen years, while I was taught at Maria Regina Roman Catholic School in Trinidad and later by the nuns of St. Angela's School in Barbados. Further similarities include that Benny Hinn was an acolyte in the Catholic Church, and so was I from age nine until twenty-four. I served as an acolyte every Sunday at St. Dominic's Church in Barbados (with the exception of two Sundays) during this fifteen year period. I was also one of the readers in Church and I took the Guild of the Archconfraternity of St. Stephen when I became a senior acolyte. I became an even stronger Catholic after

Jesus told Sister Therese that one day I would become a priest, and the nuns started calling me the *Little Bishop.* For Benny Hinn, Catholicism was his prayer life, and he practically lived at the convent of the private Catholic school he attended.

Just as all of these similarities were beginning to creep me out, Benny Hinn shared even more experiences that he had with the Holy Ghost in *Good Morning Holy Spirit,* which were very similar to ones which I had.

For instance, there was the time when the Holy Ghost was running behind Benny Hinn as he was running to get into one of his friend's car, and the Holy Ghost just got into the car after him, filling it with His glory and making Benny's friend weep in His Presence. I had a similar experience when I was at home in Barbados and was attempting to quit smoking. I ran out of the house towards my car to go and buy some cigarettes at a gas station down the road, when my mother called me back in to give me a list of items that she wanted me to collect for her from the supermarket. I heard the Holy Ghost running behind me. I could hear His footsteps. However, I stopped in my tracks and turned around too quickly, and He ran right into me, knocking me to the garage floor and slaying me in the Spirit at the same time. I was out for a few minutes.

Benny also wrote about how his Mom was cleaning the hallway outside of his room where he was spending time with the Holy Ghost and when he left the room quickly and ran into the hall, the Holy Ghost followed him quickly and knocked her down in the hallway. Similarly one night I was returning to my room at university after midnight and I was late for my date with God. There was power on the door handle and power oozing out from under the bottom of the door. I unlocked the door and opened it, only to be rushed at by the Holy Ghost, who was so happy and excited that I was there to keep my date with Him and fellowship with Him, that He ran to me and hugged me in the doorway. I was knocked out into the hallway and was slain in the Spirit for almost ten minutes.

The Holy Ghost reminded me of all of these things, one after another as I read and all I could ask Him was, "How is this possible?" and "Why was this happening to me?" I was beginning to get a little concerned because this was beyond coincidence now, this was too much for me to handle. I continued to read, only to find yet another coincidental similarity.

I had never met or seen Benny Hinn nor did I know anything about his ministry. All I knew was that in reading some parts of *Good Morning Holy Spirit* I was reading about Benny's experiences that I had experienced myself within the last two years of my life. I am not trying to boast or anything. Please don't get the wrong impression. It was quite the opposite. I was in shock. The more I read, the more in awe I became, the more I asked God how it was possible, and the more I wondered why had this happened to me. I was more worried and afraid than proud. What did it all mean? The coincidences were far too many, and they just kept on growing.

For instance, I was saved a week before Christmas 1996 on the top step of the Bible study, where I was simultaneously healed of depression. Exactly one week later—just a few days after Christmas day—I was baptized, and the next morning I had my first true face to face encounter with the Holy Ghost. These were the best Christmas presents I ever received. Similarly, Benny Hinn had his first face to face meeting with the Holy Ghost in the Christmas of 1973, which was also near to the time of his twenty first birthday. He said that the Holy Ghost was also the greatest Christmas present he ever received. His first meeting lasted eight hours while mine lasted only three. Christmas time is very special to the Father because it is the anniversary of the birth of His Son on the earth, and so He gives gifts and blessings at Christmas.

After my initial meeting with the Holy Ghost, I used to lock my door at midnight when I had a date with Him and follow His lead into glorious worship for hours—song after song, amidst steadily increasing glory filling my bedroom—while my parents were asleep in their bedroom that was directly above mine. They never knew what was happening in my room between the hours of midnight and 4 a.m. every morning when I came home on vacation. Similarly, Benny Hinn worshiped in secret behind his closed bedroom door less the events that went on behind it were discovered, and his parents did not understand what was going on in his room. They may have objected as it was not in keeping with their religious traditions.

Again the concern was raised in my mind as to why I had experienced things similar to what Benny Hinn did? This should not be happening to me. Why was this happening to me? Once again, I implored the Holy Ghost for an answer to my questions. Immediately, I got a flash in my mind of a recurring vision that I have had hundreds of times before, from the day I was saved in December 1996 to present. Day after day and night after night, I had this vision that still continues to this day.

The funny thing was that the vision predominantly occurred while I was taking a shower. You see I had set up my stereo in my bathroom and would worship the Lord along with songs on CDs, but I would only sing the songs that Jesus touched at the time. Showering was never the same again after that. In such an atmosphere the Holy Ghost would arrive in no time at all, fill my bathroom with Himself and His Glory, and touch the words of the songs.

The vision was always the same in that it was of me leading the worship of millions of people towards God and ushering them into the most intimate presence of the Holy Ghost. The very same person whom I had in my bedroom was being shared with millions the world over in huge auditoriums and vast open spaces all around the world. The thing was that the vision was always so real that I would find myself caught up in the experience. It would captivate me, and I would not only be aware of what was happening in the vision, but would also feel the intensity of the presence of the Holy Ghost in the auditorium, and the power of the glory of God as it descended on the worshipers. Whenever I was having the vision, I could stretch out my hand and feel God's power falling from the heavens like rain into the palm of my hand. I could also actually feel how tightly God's presence was packed into the auditorium, and how intense His glory was, so that the people, the worship team and the choir could no longer sing because they were overwhelmed by Him and just fell over—some of them onto their knees while others were on their faces weeping amidst His very thick Manifest Presence. Over and over again, the Holy Ghost has reiterated to me that there will be *millions* of people—never thousands, or hundreds, or hundreds of thousands—always *millions.* I have heard Him say this time and time again, year after year. As I read on, I came across a part of the book where Benny Hinn had a recurring vision of himself preaching in large open-air rallies, stadiums, and concert halls. The people coming to the services stretched as far back as the eye could see. Here we went again with more similarities with Benny Hinn.

Once again, I asked the Holy Ghost why were there similarities to begin with? What did all of this mean? Was this a glimpse of my future? What was in store for me? I was quite concerned now and wanted to know what all of this meant and what was going on. I asked the Holy Ghost over and over because I knew He was deliberately holding out on me. He was in a playful mood. He did this often with me. So I decided to play along. I implored once more, and I heard Him begin to sing,

> Que sera sera,
> Whatever will be, will be,
> The future is not yours to see,
> Que sera, sera.

I heard Him chuckle. I could not believe this. Here I was anxiously waiting for answers, and here He was teasing me. He did this all of the time. Then He approached closer to me, tapped me on my left shoulder, and whispered softly into my left ear,

"There is one body, and one Spirit…" (Ephesians 4:4). I took this to mean that the personality and characteristics of the Holy Ghost experienced by different individuals should be the same the world over. God is the same person—yesterday, today and forever—He never changes. His behavior with one person should be the same as His behavior with another.

Then I asked Him, "Why doesn't this happen to everyone?"

To which He responded, "Two weeks after you return to Buckingham, you will know."

"What is going to happen in two weeks after I return to university?" I asked anxiously, but He would not tell me anything more. However, the minute the Holy Ghost said these words to me, there was an air of excitement in the atmosphere that did not leave me until the two weeks were over. Immediately, I knew that something really big was about to happen, and I did not know what it was.

Once again it took me three days to finish it; this also meant three days of weeping in God's Presence. After completing *Good Morning Holy Spirit,* the Holy Ghost continued to be with me all day and all night long talking and walking with me all of the time. I treasured Him more than anything else in this world, and I loved spending time with Him face to face. I could never have grown tired of Him. Never. Throughout our time together however, I could feel that there was something brewing on the horizon. Something really big was about to happen, and I did not know what it was. Our fellowship continued in Leeds for the remainder of the two weeks, and then it was time to return to university.

I returned to Buckingham by coach, and that very night, I was studying in my room when the Holy Ghost appeared to me and told me to go over to the computer room in the Franciscan Building (which was open all of the time to give students internet access twenty four hours a day) and search for Benny Hinn on the internet. I locked up my room and headed out the door with the Holy Ghost walking beside me all the way to the Franciscan Building. We arrived at the computer room, and He sat beside me as I searched the internet. I quickly found Benny Hinn's website, and a quick perusal revealed that he was holding a miracle crusade or healing service at the Royal Albert Hall in London in exactly two weeks from today! Immediately, I was all excited! I thought, *This is what the Holy Ghost was referring to when He said that I will know in two weeks after I return to university. He knew about this crusade all along. If I go to the crusade I will understand why there are these similarities in experiences. London is only an hour away from Milton Keynes by train,* I thought *and I can get to Milton Keynes by taxi in thirty minutes.* The Holy Ghost told me to note down the date of the crusade and the time and the telephone number to call to order tickets. On the website I read some accounts of healings which happened at previous services, and the Lord's touch was on each of them. I logged off the computer and then realized that I did not know what Benny Hinn looked like. I did not bother to log back on to take a look because I was pressed for time as it was nearly midnight, which meant that it was time to return to my room and worship with the Holy Ghost. The Holy Ghost accompanied me back to my room, and as I stepped through the door, He began to sing. I sang everything He sang note for note and word for word, and with this, worship began.

From that night onwards, worship skyrocketed to a much higher level. I was catapulted to a more powerful, intense, and intimate level. I wondered whether it was my obedience to the Holy Ghost that night that brought this about, or whether it had something to do with the upcoming Benny Hinn Miracle Crusade. The Holy Ghost confirmed that it was both. There is always increased power and presence when I am obedient to God and when I do what He asks me to do. However, it was also a consequence of the crusade, because as the Holy Ghost said, it will be a phenomenal event where I will witness Him perform things that I would never have dreamed possible. So as the days leading up to the crusade went by, I grew increasingly more excited and so did the Holy Ghost. Frankly it was all He could talk about and all I could think about.

Every midnight He would rush into my room all excited and say, "Are you ready for the Benny Hinn crusade?"

I would check myself to see if I was all organized for the trip. "Yes, my Friend. I am all set to go." I would reply, going over all of the details in my mind. Little did I know that nothing on this earth could possibly prepare me for what I was about to experience. The excited state of the Holy Ghost increased almost exponentially every night until we went to the crusade. I had never seen Him behave like this before. He was more anxious to worship than ever before. There was more joy in the air, more power falling through the ceiling, more of His Presence than I had ever seen, He was even more excited about the crusade than I was, and I was bursting at the seams. I could not wait for the crusade.

In addition to the increased power and presence of the Holy Ghost in my room now, the mere mention of Benny's name during the two week period before the crusade was touched with Heaven's power falling from above. To hear the Holy Ghost speak about Benny brought tears to my eyes and warmth to my heart as He described him as one of his dearest, closest, and most intimate friends. The Holy Ghost spoke Benny's name with such warmth and love much like a proud father would pronounce his own son's name. It made me wonder about the depth of the relationship shared between this man and the Holy Ghost.

The very next day I called the number for Benny Hinn Ministries and reserved a ticket for myself. There was no charge for the ticket, and the person on the other end was very warm and polite. She instructed me to collect my ticket that would be waiting for me at one of the front doors of the Albert Hall before the commencement of the crusade. Later that day, I called my mother, told her about my plan to attend the crusade, and invited her to come along and meet me at the Royal Albert Hall before the crusade commenced. She said that she would have to enquire into the cost of a train ticket from Leeds to London during rush hour on a weekday, and she would base her decision on this. To be on the safe side, I booked a ticket with Benny Hinn Ministries for my mother to attend the crusade.

It turned out that the train ticket at peak time was about one hundred and forty pounds sterling. As my mother made up her mind, I eagerly made preparations over the next two weeks and organized myself as to the route I would take to get to the Royal Albert Hall. I booked a taxi from Buckingham to Milton Keynes, found out the train fare from Milton Keynes to London Euston Station, and worked out a route to get to the closest tube station to the Royal Albert Hall using the London underground system. Eventually all of the preparations for the trip to London were finalized. The taxi was booked to collect me from my dorm at 4:30 a.m., and so the night before the crusade I only worshiped with the Holy Ghost for one hour, from midnight to one o'clock in the morning. This way I could get at least three hours of sleep. However, that one hour of worship was filled with such a tremendous abundance of God's power, and such a thick mist of indescribable joy, that was God's Presence, that He quickly flooded into my room. When the Holy Ghost quickly manifested Himself in the room, He was uncontrollably excited about the crusade the following day. He could not contain Himself. Until this crusade, I did not know that God got excited about things or events. Now I knew. With my room filled with eager anticipation of all that was going to happen the next day, the Holy Ghost and I worshiped to increasingly higher levels of His Presence until it was one o'clock in the morning. Oh what glorious worship it was! It was short but powerful! When it was over, I could barely stand and keep from weeping, because His Presence was too thick—too thick even for me to stand. There was too much of Him in the room. My knees just gave way, and I flopped onto my bed. In such awesomeness I dared not speak, but I whispered my request to the Holy Ghost to wake me up at 4:00 a.m. With that I gently but quickly slipped into sleep, and as I did this, I smiled as I reflected on my past and marveled at the irony of the whole situation.

As I drifted into sleep, I hazily remembered how I would laugh at Pentecostals and Baptists when I heard them speak of healing services when I was a teenager and did not yet know the Lord. I thought that people were crazy to go to a service and let a man who I was convinced was a fake touch them and fool them into believing that they were healed of their ailments. I grew up firmly believing that such men used this ploy and the Gospel to fool hundreds of people, and to line their pockets with gold at the expense of the infirmed, and so I was the biggest skeptic when it came to healing services. However, after Jesus' power met me on the top step and healed me, I believed in God's ability to do absolutely anything. I tried to rationalize it in my mind as that was God's direct touch without the use of a man, and was convinced that I still ought to doubt any situation where a man was the go–between God and the infirmed. However, when Jesus' power met me on the top step, He not only healed me of my infirmity, put the gift of the Holy Ghost inside of me, and gave me the new birth and baptized me with the Holy Ghost, but He also converted my heart and mind. Now, no matter how hard I tried, I could not make myself doubt God. He turned the greatest skeptic into His greatest believer. I would never doubt God again. Never. Whereas in the past, I ran in the opposite direction any time I heard the words *healing service,* now here I was running to one—very anxious, excited, and eager—to see Jesus the healer, heal all ailments with His miraculous power.

"POWER! POWER! POWER!"

"POWER!" THERE IT was again. Earlier on I had heard Him in my sleep, and now that I was awake, I could hear Him say more clearly, "Power! Power! Power!" It was 4:00 a.m., and I was woken by the sound of my Master's tender but strong voice, saying one word over and over again, "Power! Power! Power! George, today you will see power!" I sat up. It was 4:00 a.m. sharp (He is always punctual to wake me), and all I could hear was "Power!" over and over again. This went on for hours. I kept asking Him what He meant by power, but His response was the same, "Power! Today you will see power!"

I hurriedly ate breakfast, showered, and ran downstairs to meet the taxi all in half an hour. I could feel God's Manifest Presence running with me towards the cab, and I could feel Him sitting in the backseat throughout the whole ride to Milton Keynes. I paid the driver and had to fight the urge to open the backdoor to let Him out. Once I entered the train station, He instructed me on how to buy a train ticket from the automated ticket teller machines, since I had never used one before. He also recommended which ticket I should buy, and He chose the departure time. Using the automated teller was not as easy as I thought. There were instructions on the machine, but they were lengthy and in fine print. Since I was pressed for time, I found it much quicker—not to mention easier—to ask the Holy Ghost to show me what to do, which He did in record time.

We got on the train together, and He began to sing songs of worship to the Father and to Jesus. He sang throughout the entire journey to London. He sat next to me during the trip, and I could feel Him leaning on my shoulder throughout the train ride. I was still very tired and kept nodding off. So I asked Him to wake me when we got to Euston Station, and I let myself succumb to sleep.

This would be two firsts for me. Except for a trip I took with my family when I was thirteen, this would be my first trip to London on my own, and my first time using the London Underground with no one but God's Manifest Presence to help me. I did not want to get lost and be late for the service, so I had already asked the

Holy Ghost to guide me every step of the way, and I had already resolved to follow Him and rely totally on Him throughout the whole journey. I was a little nervous about traveling in the vast network of tunnels of the underground. If I boarded the wrong tube, I would end up miles away from my destination and waste valuable time and money getting back to where I was supposed to be. I slept on the train regardless of my worry. My Friend would get me there; I knew He would. I just had to trust Him and do everything He told me to do. With that thought, I fell asleep. There were not many people on the train at that time, so I stretched out in my seat and made myself comfortable for the long train ride into London.

The Holy Ghost woke me just as the train pulled into Euston Station by putting His hand on my shoulder. We disembarked and took the escalator down to Euston tube station. On the tube map I located where the nearest tube station to the Albert Hall was and from my calculations it was Gloucester Road Station. So I took the Northern Line from Euston Station to Embankment where I hopped onto the Circle Line, and took the tube from there to Gloucester Road Station.

When it was time to disembark there—which I had worked out to be the closest station to the Albert Hall—the Holy Ghost prompted me, "No, not this one, get off at the next station." With His words, He gave me peace, so I stayed on the tube when it stopped at Gloucester

Road Station and got off at the next stop, which was High Street Kensington. I did this trusting that He knows better than I do, even though His instructions were contrary to the result I got when I worked it out for myself on the tube map. I walked through the tube station at High Street Kensington and climbed the stairs up to the street level, and the Hall was only a few steps away. The Holy Ghost had directed me to the tube station nearest to it just like I had asked. Had I followed my calculations and got off at Gloucester Road, I would have had a much longer walk to the Albert Hall. Oh, how I would be lost without Him!

It was now seven o'clock in the morning. It had taken me two and a half hours to get there. It was a majestic building, and it was surrounded by a large elevated pavement like a platform. Once I set foot on this raised pavement (which was also the property of the Albert Hall) the strangest thing started happening to my body—my bones started to rattle. My shoulders, arms, and legs began to vibrate in their sockets, and my teeth began to chatter. It was barely noticeable at first, but as time went on and as it got closer to nine o' clock, my bones began to vibrate more and more until I could even see them rattling in their sockets. Imagine that! In the beginning I thought it was the cold early morning temperature that had my body vibrating, but it could not have been because I was warmly clad in three layers of clothing and not in the least bit cold.

Although I was in the midst of this strange experience, I was not afraid because it was more of a funny and pleasant sensation than one to be fearful of. I vaguely remembered having a similar experience when I stood in line on the staircase outside Sister Therese's library, waiting to enter. Notwithstanding this, I still monitored the bone rattling phenomenon from time to time. So I rattled and walked around the premises looking for an open door and a line to join to collect my ticket, but it was far too early for the doors to be open. It was so early that there were only five people there at that time excluding myself. They were sitting outside one of the main entrance doors with their Bibles, chatting with one another and waiting for it to open. I went over and greeted them. They responded politely. There were two men in their twenties, two women in their twenties, and an older woman in her sixties. She was the mother of one of the younger women. The two young men were German and lived in Berlin. They had flown in the night before to attend the crusade. They were very excited and were looking forward to seeing amazing things happen at this service. They shared with me how God had their excitement growing over the last week for this miracle service, and how they could not get it out of their minds and their spirits.

Then one of them said to me with his eyes all aglow, "George, the Lord woke me up this morning with one word, one word that He has been saying over and over again."

"What word is that?" I asked, and as I asked this, all of the bones in my body began to vibrate really fast again. I held my breath in anticipation of the answer to my question. Yet somehow, I knew what the answer would be.

"Power, Power, Power. That is what the Lord woke me up saying this morning George, and He kept saying it for hours afterwards." I looked at him and smiled with my bones knocking out of control, my heart racing, and my eyes popping out of their sockets. *This was the same word which God woke me with this morning,* I thought. I was shocked that God was waking me in England and these men in Germany at the same time with the same word. I asked the men if they knew why God was saying this. They had no idea.

I stepped away from the group to have some privacy and quietly asked God what this word meant, "Master, please tell me why you woke me with the word *power* this morning?"

He quickly replied, "For I am not ashamed of the Gospel, for it is the power of God unto salvation" (Romans 1:16). Now I really needed to sit down. Too much was happening at once, and I just wanted to absorb it all and take it all in.

I sat right there on the Albert Hall steps and asked the Lord, "Jesus what does this scripture mean?"

He responded,

> Power is the litmus test for the gospel. If you have my gospel, you are sure to have God's power. A teaching without power is not my gospel. Do you remember these Scriptures?
>
> "But ye shall receive power after the Holy Ghost is come upon you ... " (Acts 1:8). "For I am not ashamed of the gospel of Christ, for it is the power of God unto salvation ... " (Romans 1:16). "Having a form of godliness, but denying the power thereof, from such turn away" (2 Timothy 3:5). "For the Kingdom of God is not in word but in power" (1 Corinthians 4:20). Power is the litmus test for the Gospel."

I understood and got up and proceeded to walk the premises because the Holy Ghost was urging me to do so. I had a sense there were things He wanted me to see. The truth is that nothing could prepare me for the events that were to occur.

I continued to walk around the premises in the direction that the Holy Ghost was leading me, until I came upon a huge bus of comparable size to those large Greyhound buses one sees in America. It had the capacity for about fifty or sixty people, and the storage space for suitcases and other luggage was in large bins at the side and at the bottom of the bus. I could see faintly through the tinted windows that the bus was filled with passengers. As it parked along the sidewalk, some of Benny Hinn's ministry officials and employees arrived and were busily scurrying around the bus. The driver descended the steps, got off the bus, and opened up all of the luggage bins under the bus, but instead of suitcases, there were wheelchairs, about fifty or sixty of them. Then eleven or twelve buses just like the first one arrived and parked. Likewise their drivers opened up their luggage compartments to reveal hundreds and hundreds of wheelchairs that they unpacked and placed on the Albert Hall pavement. Meanwhile people were going into the buses to collect their loved ones, lifting them down the stairs and placing them in their wheelchairs. Husbands were carrying their wives; sons were carrying mothers and fathers. Benny Hinn workers were carrying passengers down as well, placing them in wheelchairs, and as I watched I began to weep. I just stood there watching their plight and weeping, but I was not weeping alone. The Holy Ghost was weeping with me as He too felt very sad for them. He wrapped His arms around me in an effort to comfort me, but my heart was heavily laden and went out to them. I could not stop crying for them. I went over to a corner of the building where I could watch them undetected, and in between tears I saw their faces. Some were hopeful, some had given up, and some were just living one day at a time, while some were laughing heartily. I wept and wept. I could not stop.

I felt really sorry for these people, my throat became dry and tightly clenched, and I could not stop begging God, "Oh please, please Master, please heal them. Please! Oh, Lord ... please heal."

Then the Holy Ghost said, "Compassion. Compassion. Jesus heals because He has *compassion.*" I heard what He said, but I continued to beg Him to heal them all. There were some wheelchair occupants who looked a lot worse off than others, and as I saw them and their little disfigured bodies, I pleaded with Him even more. Some were victims of automobile accidents with scars on their faces, some were quadriplegics, and there were others who had given up all hope.

I just sat on the ground crying and begging God, "Please heal them, heal them all and don't leave any of them out." I watched what appeared to be a total of about six hundred to seven hundred wheelchairs being offloaded from the buses and their occupants being placed inside of them. The memory of these hundreds of wheelchairs lying folded on their sides, glistening in the early morning sunshine before their occupants were placed inside of them, will remain etched in my mind forever. Never in my life had I seen so many wheelchairs in one place at any one time.

I began to reason with God, "My good God, what praise will be given to you from these people if you were to heal them all? Would they ever fail to tell anyone who asks why they are no longer in a wheelchair, but instead can now walk, that You oh God did this for them?"

Immediately with power and increased presence the Holy Ghost said, "One day we will heal the lame, You and I. I will heal the lame through you. You think you have seen wheelchairs today? The days are coming when you will see thousands upon thousands and hundreds of thousands of wheelchairs, and they will all be empty because their occupants would have got up from them, walked or run away, and will never use them again."

"Oh precious Spirit, I am holding You to that promise, okay? I believe You." And with His promise to me, I felt my stomach knot untie, and the anguish in my throat muscles relax from its clenched state as I rose from the ground, following the Holy Ghost to another part of the premises.

I circled around the building and returned to the place where I had originally arrived. There was a big red London telephone booth there just like the ones you see in the movies, and the Holy Ghost said, "Go over and call Lecia's flat." I thought this was strange because left to my own devices, I would have called my mother's house to see if she had decided to come to the service or not, but I did what He said to do. Lecia answered the phone sleepily and told me that Mom had taken a train from Leeds to London a few hours ago, and hopefully would meet me outside the Albert Hall by nine o'clock. I was very happy that she decided to come because I thought that she may never have this opportunity again.

While on the phone with my little sister, I began to feel the vibration in my bones once again. As I finished the conversation and replaced the receiver upon its cradle, the vibration became stronger and stronger until my bones rattled hastily in their sockets. I folded my arms one into the other to ease the vibration, but it did not stop. Furthermore, there was a cool breeze much like air conditioning blowing throughout the property. It was there from the beginning but was undetectable because the early morning air in London was a little chilly. Now however, the sun was heating up the day; the temperature had risen and this cool wind was more noticeable blowing over the property. It was not an actual wind like a normal stream of air, but more like a coolness in the atmosphere that flowed like a strong draft of air-conditioning in specific directions. It seemed to have a mind of its own traveling wherever it wished, changing direction from time to time in any direction it fancied. This ability to change direction was also detectable. Then it happened, the vibration in my body was really strong, and I could feel the intensity of the flow of the wind growing cooler and stronger.

I had just finished speaking to Lecia when a couple of buses stopped next to the sidewalk to let off their passengers. They stopped on my side of the road only three meters away from the telephone booth that I had been using. From this very close proximity, I witnessed the strangest phenomenon I have ever seen. The passengers were about to disembark from the bus directly onto the Albert Hall pavement. Without any warning, the first passenger (an older woman) upon making contact with the pavement crumpled into a ball on the ground and just lay there twitching. This happened to the next passenger also. He stepped onto the pavement, trying to avoid stepping onto the body of the woman who lay on the ground before him. He may have thought that she was not well or that she had fainted or something to that effect. As soon as his foot touched the pavement, his leg buckled under his weight, and he fell flat onto the ground. He was out cold with no movement coming from him at all. I could not believe what I was seeing. I watched the event unfold but doubted everything as though it were merely a dream, yet the phenomenon continued to transpire right before my very eyes.

By this time the Presence of God around the bus stop was so strong that I could not help but weep until I found myself on my knees. The Holy Ghost was all around the telephone booth and the three buses. Although on my knees, I watched with eagerness and curiosity at what was happening to the disembarking passengers. One by one they proceeded to hop over the bodies crumpled on the ground, but as soon as their feet touched the pavement, they too went down. Soon the pavement was littered with bodies—some of them twitching, some completely still, some of them laughing, and some of them laughing and rolling on the pavement with what seemed to be uncontrollable joy. If I had not seen it with my own eyes, I would not have believed it, but there it was happening right in front of me to three busloads of passengers. I thought, *I wished I had brought my camera along.* One would think that after the first person went down onto the ground, then another and another; that common sense would have dictated that the passengers would have stayed in the bus and not ventured outside. But no, they persisted on disembarking as if there was something or someone attracting them off the bus. These people were falling under the power of the Holy Ghost, and there was no pastor or preacher around to cause this by laying hands on them. They were physically overpowered by His awesome Presence as they made contact with the pavement.

Throughout it all—as I watched the people on the ground—I heard the Holy Ghost say over and over again, "Peace I leave with you, My peace I give unto you, not as the world giveth, give I unto you," and later, "And the peace of God, which passeth all understanding shall keep your hearts and minds" (John 14:27 and Philippians 4:7). Now I began to understand that this is what Jesus' peace looked like—a very powerful anaesthetic with the potential to put people to sleep anywhere and anytime. Usually this power means crumpling onto the ground. I also began to ask God why these people were being slain only on the Albert Hall property and not on the other side of the road. The Holy Ghost replied by singing the hymn, "Standing on Holy Ground." Then He began to show me that Benny Hinn had rented the Albert Hall with the ministry's money, which is God's money and so today the whole building—the pavement and all of its premises—belonged to God. Consequently, His Manifest Presence was free to roam any part of it until the end of the rental period later that evening. So if any person needing help or healing stepped onto this property during this time, he or she would have encountered God's Manifest Presence walking on the premises. Nothing was affecting the people walking on the pavement of the building across the street, because God had not rented that property for the day and the Holy Ghost was not there.

The Holy Ghost continued, "For many years these people have suffered with diseases and debilitating illnesses and have come from far away, traveling for many days just to be here today. The Father knows and has seen all of this. He has heard their cries for help and seen their plight. He has seen their hope and their faith and just wanted to give them a little peace after their long journey, as if to say, you are here now; rest a while. He gives peace not as the world gives it, but a peace which passeth all understanding."

Very soon, Benny Hinn ministries staff members came running towards the bus stop and began to pick up the passengers lying on the ground and carry them into the Albert Hall. They carried them in by supporting their weight on their shoulders, and I could see the passengers staggering all over the place even though their weight was taken off their feet. They were laughing and giggling, and soon loud outbursts of laughter could be heard from some individuals. The laughter appeared to be infectious; it would move from one passenger to the staff member carrying him. Then both would start laughing, and in some cases both would even begin to stagger across the pavement. Then, the staff member would collapse on the ground under the power of the Spirit. *Incredible!* I thought.

The Spirit kept saying over and over to me as I laughed in amazement at these events, "Drunk with the new wine of the Spirit. They are drunk with the power of the Spirit because they are full of the Spirit even to overflowing" (Joel 2:19, 24 and 3:18). Then He said, "In the presence of the Lord, there is fullness of joy." The drunkenness explained their rolling around on the ground, their staggering, and their not being able to pick themselves up or walk at all. While the laughter that went on for almost half an hour was the fullness of joy that they were experiencing. I was glad for this joy because some of these people had suffered so much that they had not laughed for years.

The Spirit was now urging me to join one of the many lines that had formed at all of the entrances to the Albert Hall; of which there were quite a few around the circumference of the building. I joined one that moved fairly slowly, but everything was so exciting that I did not want to leave the outside of the Hall with all the activity going on. I could still see passengers being picked up by staff members, but the Holy Ghost was telling me to go inside the building because there were even greater things about to happen in there. So I waited in line. There was a middle aged couple standing in front of me with their Bibles in hand, and they turned around to chat with me. So did the couple behind me. Although the lines were long, the people were very friendly and had compassion for the sick and the elderly in line with them, who were still arriving for the service. They gave way to them in the line and demonstrated every type of kindness imaginable. Most people helped if assistance was needed, especially by people in wheelchairs, even without having to be asked. It was that sort of atmosphere, caring and compassionate. Jesus must have been proud of what He saw that day. I know I was. It made me proud to be a human being for the first time in my life.

While standing in line and approaching the entrance, my bones began to vibrate and rattle all over again very quickly, and it increased with intensity and frequency as I got closer to the entrance. I folded my arms one into another to hide the vibration, but it did not help. Instead people kept asking me if I was feeling cold. I just responded with a yes to avoid having to explain what was happening to me. They would probably think I was crazy if I tried to give an account of this. I wondered how many other people were having experiences similar to mine.

The line moved slowly until some of the other entrance doors to the Albert Hall were opened, and then things sped up. I was looking around for my mother but could not find her and asked the Lord to let her get there safely and very soon because it was about 8:40 a.m. I followed the line into the building, went up to the counter, received my ticket, and left the other one there for my mother, hoping she would arrive soon. I then headed to the elevator which I took to the fourth floor. These were the only seats I could get; because by the time I reserved the tickets, all of the seats on the lower floors were already taken. Furthermore by the beginning of the service, most of the seats throughout the Albert Hall were already occupied except for my mother's seat and a few others. I knew this because our seats were right at the edge of the balcony, and one could walk over to a huge brass handrail that was in front of us and look down and see all the people on every floor below. I could see the pit or ground floor and the other four floors above it. I had been told that the maximum capacity of the Albert Hall was five thousand people, which meant that each of the five floors held about one thousand people, and by the looks of it, there would be no vacant seats in the Albert Hall today.

I had asked the Lord long before ordering the tickets to orchestrate my seating. He knew something about me that I did not even know about myself, that I like to observe the movement of the Holy Ghost over a crowd of people from above, and as I look back now, I realize that He did exactly that. Being seated on the top floor at the balcony rail, I had a bird's eye view over the entire congregation.

The stage was well illuminated. I sat and waited anxiously for Benny Hinn to come onto the platform and lead worship. My bones still vibrated. Then I realized that there was a cool, wispy wind like air-conditioning flowing throughout the building, and it rose all the way to the top floor from the pit and back down again. His Presence was thick, electric, and anxious. I could feel it in my blood that this atmosphere was conducive to performing miracles, and I just sat in His Presence and wept as He grew stronger and more intense by the minute.

It dawned on me at that moment that He was at the service before Benny Hinn. He had been there since seven o'clock that morning or maybe even earlier. It is He who performs the miracles, so His Presence is necessary. Without Him at a service, no miracles will be performed. However, on the contrary, the greater His Manifest Presence, the more numerous the miracles; and the more powerfully and swiftly they are performed. I just sat there with thoughts like this flashing through my mind, receiving amazing snippets of divine revelation.

Without warning, a large man in a navy blue suit came onto the platform to lead worship. I had never seen Benny Hinn before, so I thought this was him. I stood with the rest of the congregation to worship God. There was quite an anointing on the first song, but it was considerably less on the second one. I looked the man up and down admiring his hair and his suit. I remember thinking that although he had quite a large tummy, he carried his suit off very well. He had a tremendous voice. After the second song—again without warning and very quickly—this man disappeared and on came a little man in a cream suit who spoke with a slight accent. As he came out, he hit the note of the last song we were singing with perfect pitch. I stared at him in his cream suit. I wondered, *Why cream of all colors?*

NOTHING IS IMPOSSIBLE

I OVERHEARD SOMEONE sitting behind me say to his friend, "That's Benny!" As soon as Benny Hinn came out, he started to sing a song of worship to God, and instantly the atmosphere around me became charged and electrified. All the hair on my body was standing on edge, and I could not help but stand and join in the worship. It was just too beautiful to pass up. Benny then followed the Spirit into the second song, but the touch on it was not as strong as on the first. However, with each successive song, it seemed that the power would increase until eventually we were in the midst of so much of God and His thick powerful Presence, that anything was possible; and I mean anything!

I had never seen and witnessed a miracle before—except my own healing of course—and judging from the way the day was going so far, miracles could happen at any moment. Benny started to speak about how he loves those old hymns from the past that are rarely sung today. He remarked that this crusade is being held in England, the home of these ancient hymns, and the Lord had wanted us to worship Him with them. So he burst into song with "How Great Thou Art" and flowed into and out of seven or eight more before finally reaching "Great is Thy Faithfulness." As Benny sang, the anointing grew stronger, and I began to weep. God's intimate Presence was very real that morning. The vibration of my bones and the chattering of my teeth that had stopped while we were waiting for Benny to come on, now resumed getting faster and faster as Benny progressed from song to song. It was the most glorious worship I had ever experienced.

My mother arrived and sat next to me. I kissed her and asked her about her trip from Leeds to London. We chatted about other things for a while; then I stood up and resumed worship. Within seconds, I was caught up to the heights of worship again. My mother was sitting in the seat on my left hand side while the seat to my right was vacant. I was completely enraptured by the worship, and getting higher by the minute, when an elderly lady was led by an usher to the seat on my right hand side. She sat down, and although I knew she was there, I did not remove my focus from God to greet her. I kept it on the Lord because I did not want to miss anything.

After a short while the Holy Ghost drew my attention to her white cane that she had leaned against her seat. I looked at her, smiled, and said hello, to which she responded with a polite hello back, and we chatted for a short while. During our conversation, I looked into her eyes and noticed that each one was completely covered with a thin white film, so that the lenses, pupils and irises appeared almost completely white. I could see a faint hint of her brown pupils peeking through the nearly opaque film. Whatever this was, it must have significantly affected her vision, but as to whether it caused total blindness, it was difficult to tell.

By this time a few healings had already happened to people in their seats. God healed them in their seats. The Holy Ghost would go over to people during the service, touch them, heal them, and make them whole. Merely standing in God's Manifest Presence can make a person's body whole. This is the method of healing that God uses at Benny Hinn's services and crusades today, which He also used at Kathryn Kuhlman's services many years before. Benny and Kathryn are the vessels which have been cleaned by God and are used to usher in the Manifest Presence of God into the auditorium or location of the service. The Holy Ghost's Presence is ushered in when the vessel—Benny or Kathryn—worships God singing the songs He asks them to sing until He enters the building. Once He arrives, He goes to people in their seats and touches them—healing them, repairing broken bodies, and curing supposedly incurable diseases. This is a very different modus operandi from a preacher laying hands on the sick and healing them. God uses it because it is far more efficient for an omnipresent God to touch and heal fifty or sixty people at a time, and work His way through an entire football stadium full of people, than for a man to lay hands on one sick person at a time until the whole stadium is done.

Actually, at the end of the service, I found out that some healings even occurred before the service began. They happened on the very anointed premises of the Albert Hall as God the Holy Ghost walked upon it for two hours before the service that day. The mere fact that He trod upon the premises made it holy ground just for that day, and as the sick trod upon the Albert Hall grounds, they were made well. Not because of the property itself but because of His Manifest Presence on the property. As He went to the sick, the Holy Ghost touched them, making them well. People shared with me how they felt a soothing warmth on the affected parts of their bodies that took their pain away or ended their bleeding, and afterwards, they reported a wonderful coolness over the once affected area or over their entire body. The next step was to go to their doctor to verify their healing.

Some healings even happened as people left home with the intention of attending the service. They either felt tremendous warmth over their ailing limbs or diseased organs or over their entire body, and then their pain dissipated never to return again. I was shocked as I was told of these accounts by the very people who had experienced these healings.

The healings that happened in the seats were brought to everyone's attention because the recipients were shouting for joy—one by one in the Albert Hall as they felt God touch them—like people exclaiming "Bingo!" in a bingo hall. It was funny at first, but then as it started to happen more often, I realized what in fact was really happening. God was bringing to an end the agony and suffering that these people had endured for years.

Then the worship began to climb higher and higher, taking me to heights of worship that I have never experienced before nor thought possible until now. The power and Presence of God was so strong that I wept uncontrollably, and my bones were vibrating faster than ever before. As we went from hymn to hymn in reverent succession, God's power and Presence intensified until it was unbelievable, from "How Great Thou Art" to "Great is Thy Faithfulness" to "All Hail the Power of Jesus' Name," until we reached the pinnacle of worship where the power was just amazing. I worshiped with all of my heart and realized that we had plateaued at this pinnacle (or at this highest point of worship) and that He was very thickly concentrated throughout the building.

In fact we were in the midst of so much of God, and His thick powerful Presence, that miracles could happen at any moment. Nothing was impossible. Anything could happen at any time, and I knew it. I knew that at this moment hundreds of people in the Albert Hall were being healed in their seats from their ailments and diseases. Hundreds! Every part of me knew this. The Holy Ghost told me so. Now was the time when God was doing the majority of His healing work. Like little explosions scattered throughout the Albert Hall, people were healed quickly, powerfully, and to the undiscerning eye, it would appear to be randomly. He started with twenty at a time, scattered throughout the building…then fifty…then hundreds! Hundreds of mini–explosions in the bodies of people were set off at the same time in multiple locations throughout the Albert Hall, as only an almighty omnipresent God can do.

The numbers of the healed grew steadily. The Holy Spirit continued showing me this along with the mechanism of the healing, which begins with great warmth surrounding and covering the affected area of the person who is being healed, whether it be an organ, bone, or muscle. If bones are broken or malformed, the person will first experience the anaesthetized state of being filled with God's peace unto overflowing, which is God administering His powerful anesthetic before performing a painful procedure (John 14:27 and Philippians 4:7). Sometimes in addition, the person will also be tipsy or inebriated with the new wine of the Spirit that He pours out onto the person, so that they do not feel pain when the Holy Spirit starts to physically realign their malformed or deformed bones, or to fuse broken ones back into position (Joel 2:19,24 and 3:18). Such persons are usually seen staggering and laughing incessantly. Then this cool Wind or breeze begins to flow around the affected area completing the healing and giving long–awaited joy to the individual who has suffered for so long. This joy also ensures that they feel no pain after the bone realignment or other painful procedures have been completed.

The ears of the deaf experience the warmth of God's touch, and their ears pop open, as do the eyes of the blind feel His warm hands upon their eyes just before their sight is restored. Then the cool Wind surrounds them, and if they are to experience salvation, the Wind enters in through their nostrils and their mouths. God breathes into them, leaving within their bodies the deposit of Himself which is the gift of the Holy Spirit. This re-establishes the supernatural link and Spirit connection with God the Father and Jesus that Adam had in the garden of Eden before he disobeyed God. From that moment onward, that person is not just healed of their ailment but is born again of the

Holy Ghost, has God's seal within him forever, and will live with Jesus in His Kingdom for all eternity.

Most people who experience salvation also get healed of their ailment. Most times, the ailment comes as a result of satan knowing that this person's pre-destined time for salvation is very soon, and he does everything in his power to make that person's life very uncomfortable, akin to a living hell. So a few months before their salvation date, the person comes down with an ailment that could just be a nuisance designed to prevent the individual from getting to the crusade, where he would meet God and experience salvation and healing. Sometimes satan sends a life threatening disease, but this too is healed in the same way. That is on the day of salvation when salvation and healing are experienced simultaneously. This is because when a person gets saved, God places Himself into them, and the illness must leave, since satan must leave. For those who have been ill for years, a curse has been placed on them by satan, and as God puts Himself into them, the curse will be broken instantly as God takes over and satan is forced to let go. For those who are not healed but are only saved, God will require faith on their part if they are to obtain their healing. This faith is biblical faith or Greek faith.

Healing by faith or believing God's *rhema* or God's spoken Word has been going on for centuries since Jesus died on Calvary where it became our reality that "By his stripes we are healed" (Isaiah 53:5).

I looked over at my mother and she was weeping as the Presence of God overwhelmed her. I looked over at the lady next to me. She was in her seat talking to someone, but there was no one visibly present. I assumed she was talking to the Lord. I got a sense that she was asking Him to heal her eyes. I felt sad for her because the healings were over. Or at least so I thought. Little did I know what God had in store. The deep silence ended, and Benny began to sing very softly at first,

> He Touched Me! ... Oh, He Touched Me! ...
> Oh the joy that filled my soul.
> Something happened and now I know
> He touched me and made me whole.

The power of God filled the building again and the Spirit of God urged me to look over to the woman once again. She was crying and the more the congregation sang "He Touched Me;" the more she cried. She cried and cried. She wept uncontrollably as she looked down at her hands, turned them over, and looked at them again. My jaw dropped. I thought, *Did she just look at her hands?* Doubt set into my mind immediately.

She sat in her seat talking to Jesus. I could hear her. For about half an hour, she just sat there in communion with Him—just Him and her alone—thanking Him for giving her sight. With tears of gratitude that flowed down her cheeks and fell onto her seat, she thanked Him from the bottom of her heart. She looked in my direction and smiled as did I. I think she was a little embarrassed and was looking around to see who had seen what had happened. My eyes met hers, and I smiled reassuringly to comfort her. The white film that previously covered her eyes was gone. I could see her brown pupils now very clearly for the first time. I was shocked at what I was seeing.

In the midst of all of this, I could feel the intensity of the power falling on her because now it began to fall on me too. From the moment my eyes took in what had happened to her, the power moved from her to me and incorporated me into what was happening to her. I was immediately filled with wonder and amazement at what had obviously happened and began to share in what must have been for her, unbelievable joy! The power fell with great force for about twenty to thirty seconds, and as I looked at her, I could see that she was enjoying it too. When the power stopped falling, she folded her white cane, put it into her handbag, looked right at me, made eye contact, and smiled. I smiled back. She continued to smile, holding back the tears which were still trickling down her cheeks. "Tears of gratitude," I heard the Holy Ghost say. Then she stood up, headed towards the elevator, entered it, and disappeared. I knew what had just happened, but I could not let myself believe what I had just seen.

In fact at that point, I doubted what I had witnessed first hand, and my mind questioned it. So I asked God,

"Lord if this woman really was blind to begin with and if she really was healed, then show me. Prove to me that You healed her."

The worship continued, and those who were healed began to form lines to go up onto the platform to give thanks and to share their testimonies with Benny and the congregation. The lines were beginning to get long, and since I was more interested in the worship, that is what I continued to do. Then my mother had to leave. She was meeting Lecia at 2 p.m. in Leeds, so she had to leave now if she was to meet her on time. I kissed her goodbye and watched as she too disappeared into the elevator.

I watched as people went up onto the platform—one by one to share how God had healed them of terrible illnesses and debilitations only hours before. Some were paraplegics confined to wheelchairs, which were now walking and later on running around the platform. Some were cancer patients, leukemia sufferers, who were all claiming they felt a warmth come over their affected areas that were once painful but now were painless.

Then I saw her. She was next in line, and there was a sudden hush. The Holy Ghost nudged me to get my attention. It was the little woman who had sat next to me throughout the healing service. She was in the line about to go up the stairs onto the platform. She had a few people in front of her in the line. From that distance she was easily recognizable in the long black dress she was wearing. Soon it was her time to go onto the platform.

As she was approaching Benny Hinn on the platform, one of his junior pastors relayed the history of her illness to the congregation. She was originally from Jamaica but had been living in England for many years. Her vision began to be impaired two years ago by a thick white growth covering the lenses of her eyes. Her doctor diagnosed her as suffering from cataracts in both eyes, and she could not afford the surgery to remove them. Instead she had turned to God asking Him to remove them. In the meantime, she had lost all vision in her left eye and about 90 percent in her right eye and was forced to learn how to get around with her cane. Jesus was her only hope for recovery, and He had come through for her. She had walked into the Albert Hall using her cane and led by an usher, and now she was going to walk out without either of them. How wonderful!

"Thank You Jesus," was all she said over and over again. "Thank You Jesus for giving me my eyes back." She began to cry again—overwhelmed at the miraculous gift which had been given to her—at no cost to her, just freely given. Benny was noticeably moved also.

Then at that moment power fell upon me, on no one else but me, and all of a sudden I understood what it was like to be in her shoes with her helplessness and her hope. She had been crying to Jesus for help, but nothing could prepare her for the miraculous. I felt her shock at being able to see. I cried because I understood. At that moment I understood. All I could do then was bow my head and kneel before God and apologize, "Thank You Lord for your confirmation. I will never doubt You again. Never."

Benny Hinn was moved by her plight and asked her what she thought of being able to see again, and of all the things and people she had not seen for such a long time and was now seeing again. She was still crying when she replied, "Beautiful! Beautiful! Everything and everybody is so beautiful!"

THE PROMISES

THE BLIND WOMAN'S testimony went right through me as God made sure the reality of the miracle hit home, making me come to grips with the fact that He can make the impossible an everyday reality. I watched as more people joined the lines to go up onto the platform and share their testimonies of healing with the rest of the congregation and Benny Hinn. There were so many testimonies of healing that this segment went on for nearly an hour.

A middle–aged European woman came up, who also had cataracts in both eyes that the Holy Ghost had removed during the worship segment of the service. (I saw her again at a Benny Hinn crusade in Amsterdam Holland in 1999, hopping onto the bus I was taking to the Amsterdam crusade. Her eyes were obviously healed as she jumped on and off the bus effortlessly without needing assistance. I noticed it immediately and remarked upon it to her. Her response was a quick one with a smile, "To God be all the glory." She marveled at the fact that I was at the Albert Hall service when God had restored her sight and that I had remembered her ailment in the midst of so many people who were healed at the crusade.)

There was a little boy, who had been born with deformed legs and needed leg braces to walk, but now he was walking—in fact running on the platform without his braces, and Benny stooped down and hugged him obviously overwhelmed. I cried openly when I saw this as God promised me over and over, "You too shall do this.

You too shall do this."

Then there was a little girl who was born deaf, and Benny Hinn had all of the microphones turned off except his own, which he placed in front of the little girl's mouth while whispering into her ear, "Say Jesus."

"Jesus!" she replied.

Again he said, "Say Jesus."

"Jesus!" she replied. I wept and so did the whole congregation who willingly joined in applauding God for the misfortunes–turned–into–victory stories in the lives of the people on the platform. There was a genuine outpouring of joy by the crowd for the recipients of the miraculous healings who were on the platform. Power was still falling like rain. By now the top portion of my shirt was fairly damp from my tears, notwithstanding that I could not stop myself from weeping under God's unceasing power. I did not care anymore; I was undone by what I was witnessing and so were many others. I could tell from looking around amongst the crowd and seeing their jaws dropped in awe at some of the miraculous healings that took place. The congregation exploded with thunderous applause to the God of compassion. It was too much to handle, too overwhelming. *What a good God You are,* was all I could think, and all the while the Holy Ghost was saying, "You too shall do this."

Testimony after testimony of each healing was shared with the congregation until there were no more. Throughout this segment, the power of God continued to fall in the building. However, it did not fall continuously like it did throughout the worship segment. Instead it fell when specific testimonies were being shared which He Himself bore witness to by raining down His power. The testimonies were amazing, and in some circumstances mind boggling. Anyone who has been ill could empathize with the sick people there and be jubilant along with them when they were healed and made better, especially in such miraculous ways. Most of them were singing the hymns to God when they felt God touch and heal them. Others were just sitting down and looking at what was going on in the service when they started to feel the heat of the Holy Ghost on the affected parts of their bodies, only to realize moments later that they too were healed.

Many of them—seeing others who were worse off than themselves—began asking God to heal them meanwhile forgetting about their own illnesses, when suddenly they received their own healing. The Holy Ghost told me afterwards that this was one of the keys to healing.

Benny Hinn recommenced worship, and within minutes the atmosphere was charged again. But this time there was more of God's Presence than His power. Benny went from song to song as the Holy Ghost led him. The air became more electrically charged, and more of God's Presence began to fill the building. It was as though He was packing as much of Himself into the Albert Hall as He could, in the same way that His train filled the temple which Solomon had built for Him. There was so much of His Presence now that He appeared as a cloud of dense matter that aberrated the light rays emitted from the lights in the Albert Hall, and so distorted my vision much like a mirage does on a hot steamy day. The more we sang, the more of Himself God seemed to be packing into the Albert Hall, and when I was beginning to think that there was no more of Him that could fit, He would pack even more of Himself into the building.

By this time, Benny was singing softer, almost whispering, and the congregation followed him in lowering the volume of their voices to sing in soft whispers also. At this point I could barely move and so it was with everyone else, because God had packed Himself all around me, tightly encompassing me and everyone else in the Hall. I remember taking my right hand and waving or sweeping it in the air in front of me with my fingers closed and feeling that I was pushing against some form of substance and matter in the atmosphere. Then I opened my fingers and realized that I had God—the Holy Ghost's matter or whatever substance He was made from—passing in between my fingers.

I remember being so completely encircled by God that I asked Him if I could touch Him. Over and over I asked Him, "Can I touch You? Please can I touch You?" Then just as I was asking for this, Benny asked the congregation to raise their hands and to continue to worship God. I raised my hands, and to my surprise I felt this cooler wind blowing amidst and around my fingertips. It was almost as cold as ice. I retracted my arms, and my fingers became warm again. Slowly, I put my hands back into the air where this cold stream of air circulated and danced amongst my fingers, which became cold again. I left my hands in the air as it was a very pleasant sensation. From my wrists down to my body, I was cool; but from my wrists to my fingertips, I was almost ice cold. Benny again told the congregation to raise their hands and to continue to worship God, which I did. Once again I felt this cooler Wind blowing through my fingertips and God's matter pressing against me from all around.

This was the most of God that I had seen in the building. In fact it was the most of Him I had ever seen, *period.* There was so much of God in the building at that moment that I was afraid to speak and afraid to worship. Immediately, all worship ceased. Benny was silent—dead silent. God was in the building. All of Him! I was awe–struck. Speechless. I did not know what to do. I just stood very still. Then He moved.

Benny breathed into the microphone with gusto. One sharp, short breath and five thousand people were pushed backwards onto the ground by a powerful invisible force.

When Benny breathed into the microphone, a strong fast moving Wind pushed the matter or substance all around us, which in turn pushed the entire 5,000 strong congregation onto their backs and onto the ground. While this was happening, I stood on the balcony holding firmly to the big brass rail in front of me, in a futile effort to prevent myself from falling under God's power, and from being blown over by the Wind. I watched from my bird's eye view above the crowd, as this powerful Wind blew from the front of the Albert Hall where Benny was standing, knocking over successive rows of the congregation on all five floors with a domino effect—all the way to the back of the building. It was amazing to watch and wonderful to experience. The first row fell first, then the second and the third, then the fourth, fifth and sixth, all the way to the last row. From my vantage point, it looked like a Mexican wave sweeping right through the building and leaving no one standing in its wake. I was in shock, very surprised, but very impressed. Never before had I ever experienced such a powerful invisible force. Although invisible, the Wind and force were tangible, and regardless of how tightly I clung to the brass rail, I was bowled clean off my feet and before I knew it, plastered to the floor. I tried to stand up, but my legs were limp and so were my arms and the rest of my body.

I just lay there on the ground in a state of rest. For the first time in months, I had perfect peace. "And the peace of God, which passeth all understanding..." I heard the Holy Ghost say. I pushed myself over to the balcony rail and found myself laughing and others were laughing too—almost uncontrollably. I just wanted to stop worrying about life's concerns and difficulties and to sit back and laugh.

Then I heard the Holy Ghost say, "In the presence of the Lord there is fullness of joy." I reached up from the floor for the rail and pulled myself up, looking over the balcony at the 5,000 below. There was not one person standing. Everyone was flat on their backs resting. 1,000 people in the pit as well as 1,000 on each of the four floors of the Albert Hall. The place looked like a disaster area, like a hurricane just blew through it.

Everyone had been blown over by this strong Wind and the direction of the Wind could be seen very clearly. It started from the front where Benny was on the platform and moved with a powerful force to the back of the building. It maintained this direction on every floor throughout the building, leveling the crowd as it passed by. Then a really strong and intimate Presence of God's train re-collected, filling the temple, and He was all over the building again as if what went before was just a taste of greater things to come.

Benny again said, "Stand up and raise your hands to the Lord." Needless to say, only about half of the congregation obeyed his instructions. Only half could. The rest of them were flat on the floor either sound asleep, drunk in the Spirit, or giggling funnily with great big smiles on their faces (Acts 2:15–18). As for me, I held tightly to the balcony rail with both arms and pulled my body up to an almost standing position only to find that there was an awesome hush, and the atmosphere was again packed to the hilt with God's matter. Benny breathed quickly into the microphone, and I held firmly to the balcony rail, readying myself to brave the powerful Wind–which evident from the heads of people falling hard before me–was heading straight for me. I watched as this powerful yet sweet Wind began to blow people over on all of the floors once again. They were literally blown over by God until no one remained standing. It was wonderful to watch as God moved over everyone in the crowd below. I kept my arms firmly wrapped around the balcony rail as the mighty Wind came upon me. I could feel the cool rushing Wind pushing against the matter around me with tremendous force, and the matter in turn was pushing me over backwards. The Wind pushed silently with great force. All that was heard was the sound of bodies hitting the floor, and the exclamations of people caught off guard, expressing their surprise as they were tumbled over by its might. I too would have keeled over had I not anchored myself to the balcony rail. I was once again surprised at the speed and the tremendous force with which this Wind executed its job. It was akin to trying to stand upright with hurricane force winds blowing from all around, and for the first time, I understood how the Holy Ghost entered the upper room like a mighty rushing Wind at Pentecost. Now it all made sense to me as I was now experiencing it. I never understood how that happened until now, as it became reality to me as I clung to the brass rail trying to remain upright and not keel over like the rest of the congregation. However, I was not strong enough, and my legs were tired from standing for the five hours of worship and eventually gave way under the force of the Wind and the pressure of my weight. On my way down—just before crashing to the ground—I caught a glimpse of the floors below and the number of people who were now motionless on the ground, and my eyes popped out of their sockets in amazement. I thought, *What tremendous power You have!*

I remember telling God in my awe struck state, "Wow! What power You possess!

I have never seen anything like this. You are so great! I must have this! I must have this!" I exclaimed over and over. "All that I have seen here today ... please grant that I may have it all!" I begged God. Then I continued, "Before today I did not know what I wanted to do with my life, but now that I have seen this, I know my heart will never let me forget it, and I will implore God until it is my life. I would love to spend my days leading worship to God in mass crusades all over the world. It entails the same basic principle of worshiping my Father and Jesus while being led by You, my Manifest Presence of God, singing song after song in my bedroom, which You and I have been doing every midnight for nearly two years now at Bucks. From my bedroom to the platform! That was all the job required!" I exclaimed. *I was already qualified for the job,* I thought. *How I loved those intimate midnight hours of worship!*

Then the Holy Ghost began to sing to me, "I was made to worship You ..." The words of the song describe how I was designed and constructed for the sole purpose of worshiping Him, and the more He sang it to me, the more I realized what He was trying to get me to understand. My Father designed me for this sole purpose, and I did not know it until now. I was made to lead mass congregations into God's innermost intimate Presence where miracles happen ... where the sick are healed ... where there is salvation ... and to teach people to obtain God's Manifest Presence for themselves. This way they can have Him in a physical and tangible way in their lives, and He can have a deeper relationship with them. (This is the very purpose of this book.) This is why I loved worship so much and had this craving for the Holy Ghost for all of these years.

Now all of the pieces of the puzzle fitted together perfectly, and for the first time in my life, I saw very clearly my destiny and my calling. Everything in my life now made sense to me, and the Holy Ghost reminded me very quickly of things past. He reminded me of Sister Mary Therese—the librarian and my teacher of religious knowledge—who when I was nine years old was told three times by Jesus that one day—I would be a priest. For an entire two year period, she held firm to what He told her and reminded me over and over of what He said. She was the first encounter I had with a person to whom Jesus spoke. I had interpreted this to mean a Catholic priest, but she never elaborated; and I never pursued the matter, dreading the thought of a life of celibacy and poverty. Now here I was—eighteen years later—asking Jesus to be a priest of the order of Melchizedek, one who worships God in Spirit and in truth and a minister to Him and to His Bride. Then the Holy Ghost reminded me how difficult and demanding I had found high school, and was at present finding university, because these institutions wanted me to choose a career and choose appropriate subjects at *O* level and again at *A* level towards attaining that goal. Yet none of my options felt right. With every choice I made and with every subject I chose, I had no peace in my mind or spirit, causing me to be a troubled teenager and uneasy throughout my student days. This eventually caused me to change my choice of career at the time from medicine to law. It all did not matter anymore because high school and university cannot prepare anyone for this kind of profession—only the Holy Ghost and the anointing can.

I was so happy and my spirit was settled for the first time in my life that I was going to be a "professional evangelist" as the Holy Ghost called it. What that really meant I did not know, but the Holy Ghost then gave me the name of the ministry, *Holy Ghost Ministries.* It would be His ministry—devoted to Him, named after Him, performed for love of Him, and the miracles performed by Him. I was very happy and held these things dear to my heart, asking Him to remind me of all these things when I got home so that I could write them all down.

I was still in such awe at God's demonstration of power that I just lay there on the floor staring up at the ceiling in wonder asking myself, *how powerful was God, really?* I thought I knew Him and all of His capabilities, but now I had to admit to myself that in reality I did not. I had put Him in a box and limited Him. Once I admitted this and apologized to Him for doing so, that was when it all started.

The Holy Ghost said, "George, ask for whatever you wish. Now is the time to ask. If you ask Jesus for whatever you wish now, especially the innermost desires of your heart, you shall have them, every single one of them."

"Precious One, I don't know what I want, and I definitely don't know what desires lurk in the innermost recesses of my heart." I replied. With that He began to prod me incessantly, asking me to let Him show me what desires lay deep inside my heart and saying that He would pray and intercede for me to the Father and to the Son on my behalf. Throughout all of this, I had been lying flat on my back on the floor, but now I was pulling myself up using the railing and peering over the balcony to see what was going on below. People were still not moving in the pit; they were all flat on their backs laughing or sleeping. Power fell upon me, infilling me as I now beheld the effects of this awesome Wind. Just at that moment and to my utter astonishment, the very words of the Holy Ghost came out of Benny's mouth.

I could not believe my ears; almost word for word, Benny said, "Saints now is the time to ask Jesus for whatever you wish. If you ask Him for whatever you wish now, especially the innermost desires of your heart, you shall have them, every single one." I froze, and every hair on my body stood on end. How uncanny! God had said the same thing twice in two minutes—once personally to me and then again through Benny. This was grounds to take God very seriously. Never had I had such a sense of urgency to ask quickly before the opportunity was lost and before the window closed forever. I got a sense it was only open for a short while. The Holy Ghost was waiting for me to make my move, and He would not let me stand up completely until I did.

I said, "Holy Ghost I don't know what to pray for, this is all new territory to me, so please lead me in prayer. You take over, show me what to pray for, and intercede for me." Quickly, He began to give me a sense of what I was to pray for, and I just followed Him. I prayed aloud to the Father and to Jesus. I said,

> Father I am hungry for all that You, Jesus, and Your Holy Ghost have to offer. Before today, I did not know what I wanted to do with my life. I don't know if I would ever practice law, I am no good at it, and I don't love it. All I love is You; all I enjoy doing is spending time with You, worshiping You and fellowshipping with Your Manifest Presence. You are all that I have, and all that I really want in this life. So I am elated that You have promised me that I will be a *professional evangelist.* Thank You—but if I am going to travel the world and preach and teach

> Your Gospel—I humbly ask You to equip me with Your awesome power. Please let Your power accompany me to the maximum it can be.

Immediately the Holy Ghost told me what I should ask the Father and Jesus for. I continued in obedience to Him, putting my feelings aside, because time was of the essence, "I humbly ask for the maximum amount of Your power possible that I can hold without dying. More power and anointing than I have even seen and experienced here today! It is crazy to ask for this Father!" I said to Him aloud, "but this is what the Holy Ghost is instructing me to ask for." I nodded my head in disbelief. I could not believe what I was being told to ask for. Immediately as I made the request to the Father and to Jesus, power fell on me from above with tremendous force, and I was infilled. So I said it again, "Precious Jesus, I ask you for the maximum amount of anointing and power possible—when we go into Your ministry—many thousands times the portion of power that I have witnessed here today."

Immediately the Holy Ghost responded, "I am not ashamed of the Gospel for it is the power of God..." Once again power fell through the ceiling like Niagara Falls onto and into me when He spoke. Now it felt right inside of me to ask for this. Immediately the Holy Ghost said, "It shall be given to you just as you have requested. You shall have all that you wish."

Ever since I read *Good Morning Holy Spirit* the first time, I admired Benny Hinn. To me, he was the most powerful man of God alive in the world in this century. He has the Holy Ghost manifested in every service, performing wonderful miracles and demonstrating God's awesome power; but more importantly to me, he had the Manifest Presence of the Holy Ghost personally and shared intimate moments with Him on a daily basis. I thought very highly of this man of God, and there was a soft spot in my heart for him because God had used him to teach me how to get His Manifest Presence in my life daily and how to keep Him. Now I thought to myself, *How crazy I was to ask for such a thing, and how pompous of me to ask for it as well.* I felt ashamed at what I had just asked God for. But nevertheless, it was what the Holy Ghost had commanded me to ask Jesus for; and regardless of how I felt about it, I had to obey Him. I did have God's affirmation twice with power that He would grant the request, but I still felt unworthy to ask for it. Left to my own devices, my feelings of unworthiness and my low self-esteem would have got in the way, and I would never have asked God for this. Never! After all, I was requesting a lot of power, and *who am I* that I should ask for such a mighty thing as this.

The clock was still ticking, and I only had a limited amount of time left to ask God for whatever else I wanted. I searched my heart for something else that

I wanted in my life, but could think of nothing. In my spirit I knew that I was leaving out something even more important than power, but what was it? I asked myself. Then with the speed of lightning the Holy Ghost reminded me that I had left out the most important Person in my life ... Him.

"ONE THING HAVE I DESIRED OF THE LORD . . . THAT I MAY DWELL . . . "

I COULD NOT help but feel that time was of the essence, and it was running out. The window would remain open for only a short while more, and then it would be closed forever. So I hurried to get all of my requests in before that happened. Again the Holy Ghost nudged me to ask the Father for something, but this time it was something far more important and far more precious than all that had been requested so far.

So again I asked Him, "Precious Holy Ghost, show me what else to request from my Father; because like before, I don't know what my innermost desires are or what I should ask for." Immediately He began showing me something that I did not know and which I had never heard any preacher or teacher explain before.

He said, "One thing have I desired of the Lord, that will I seek after, that I may dwell in the House of the Lord all the days of my life, to behold the beauty of the Lord and to inquire in His temple" (Psalms 27:4). As the Holy Ghost said these wonderful words, my eyes were opened, and for the first time ever, I saw the meaning of David's Psalm 27. Instantly, I understood what David was writing about. The Holy Ghost had so clearly revealed it to me that I was left speechless. I saw that David loved God's Manifested Presence so much that he wanted one thing above all. That is to live with the Holy Ghost in the place of His abode on the earth. In David's time, God's Manifest Presence lived in the holy of holies of the tabernacle that is found past the outer court... past the holy place... past the veil into the holy of holies. Here the Ark of the Covenant was kept that held Moses' Ten Commandments and Aaron's rod that budded. God the Holy Ghost—the third Person of the Trinity, who is God's Manifest Presence on the earth—sat upon the mercy seat of the Ark of the Covenant and lived there. This was His dwelling place, His place of abode or permanent address on the earth, and David wanted to live there too. No more would he be satisfied with only weekly or daily visits from God (or as in my case, nightly visits from Him at midnight). Now

David could have Him—twenty four hours a day, seven days a week—all the days of his life because he was now living where God lived, a permanent resident of the holy of holies.

Quickly, the Holy Ghost showed me that the effect of living in God's house is really the motive for asking to live there in the first place. He showed me that the longing and desire to have more of the Holy Ghost's appearances, company, and fellowship was the reason why David made this request to live in God's house to begin with. Probably, he missed the Holy Ghost, and he was experiencing one of those lonely moments when He was not around. Probably, he was waiting for that special time of the day when God would appear to him daily and fellowship with him. Maybe, he just wanted more of his Friend. I don't know; all I know is that three hours a day were not enough anymore. He wanted Him twenty four hours a day because he missed his Friend so much when He was not around. This was the reason why David asked God to dwell in His dwelling place, to move into His House (or apartment) if you will.

Once a man has tasted the sweet and fulfilling fellowship of God's Manifest Presence, it is impossible not to want more of Him. So the man will thirst after His Presence until he has Him all to himself—all the time, all the days of his life. It is only a matter of time before the thirst takes over. So it was with David, and so it was now also with me.

Once David got into God's house, God would be around him all of the time because he was constantly in God's space. Like a houseguest who is sharing cramped quarters in the home of his host will frequently bump into the host, and the two will continuously be around each other and be forced to share the limited space with each other, so also would the Holy Ghost consistently occupy the proximate physical space of any person who dwells in His House.

One of the many effects of living with God is that He walks with you wherever you go, and you can walk with Him wherever He goes. There is a hymn called "The Garden" that goes,

> And He walks with me and He talks with me
> And He tells me I am His own,
> And the joy we share as we tarry there
> None other has ever known.

He is forever talking to you and appearing to you, so you will never pine for Him or be without Him ever again.

Also, I don't know what happened to the Ark of the Covenant. To this day, there is an ongoing debate as to its present location, but what I do know is what the Holy Ghost showed me. He said that when Jesus was being crucified at Calvary—at the instant when He gave up the Ghost—the veil which marked the entrance to the holy of holies was torn in two from top to bot-

torn by the Holy Ghost from the inside, marking a turning point for all mankind. Before Jesus' crucifixion, the holy of holies could only be visited one day a year (Yom Kippur or the Day of Atonement) by the high priest after he had performed ceremonial washings and had been purified for this purpose. The purified high priest would have a rope tied around his ankle, and he would go behind the veil to sprinkle bullock's and goat's blood onto the mercy seat of the Ark of the Covenant to make atonement for the sins Israel committed during the past year. If the priest was not satisfactorily pure, he died instantly on entering the holy of holies, and this is where the rope came in. It was used to get his corpse back out by pulling him out from behind the veil and past the holy place, back into the outer court, by the remaining priests in the outer court. Likewise if the high priest went into the holy of holies on any day other than the Day of Atonement, he would meet the same fate. So to have God's Manifest Presence everyday for the rest of a man's life was very, very rare.

However, Moses had His Manifest Presence for many days at a time, David dwelt where He dwelt, Samuel slept next to the Ark of the Covenant as a young boy in the temple, and maybe there were others who had Him for extended periods of time. I don't know. From the instance of Jesus' death at Calvary and the tearing of the veil at the entrance to the holy of holies from top to bottom, God's Manifest Presence was no longer restricted to live on the Ark behind the veil and to only fellowship with the high priests. The Holy Ghost was now allowed to fellowship with all born again believers of Jesus on the earth if they would have Him. Before His death, Jesus told His disciples that He must go so that the Counselor or the Holy Ghost may come, which He did as tongues of fire and then He proceeded to inhabit the new temples (or tabernacles) which are the human bodies of men who would accept Him into their lives. Remember Jesus said, "The kingdom of God is within you." (Luke 17:21). In addition to this, His Manifest Presence appeared, spoke to, and led these new temples that were now inhabited by the gift of the Holy Ghost.

Paul wrote in 2 Corinthians 13:14 that he wished, "The grace of our Lord Jesus Christ, and the love of God, and the *communion of the Holy Ghost* be with you all."

This meant that Paul used to fellowship with God's Manifest Presence also. The Holy Ghost did not only live in him but also would appear to him externally and *commune* with (or fellowship) with him.

All of the above information flashed through my spirit and my mind in the twinkle of an eye, and the Holy Ghost left me in a state where I felt my head would explode, because of the rapid inflow of information that had just flooded my spirit. However, now I knew what He wanted me to ask the Father for. So I began verbalizing the innermost desires of my heart that I neither had the knowledge of, nor the courage to express until today,

> Dear Father, I humbly ask You to set a fire in my heart that will never be extinguished, to remain in love with the Holy Ghost, and to want more and more of Him as each day passes. I am afraid that I will die without having all of the Holy Ghost and experiencing all of his Manifest Presence in my life. I would like to have Him all to myself in a deeper and more personal way than ever before. So I ask You for more of Him and from what You have just shown me, there is so much more of Him yet to be experienced. I beg You to make us inseparable and to make us one that we may be one as You and Your Son are one, and You and the Holy Ghost are one, because I cannot live without Him. I must have more of Him. I have tried to be apart from Him, and I cannot do it—not for one second, not for one moment of the day—because my heart pines for Him. To have Him at every service when we go into ministry is not enough. I must have Him all of the time—to talk to and to walk with hand in hand—every minute of every day of my life for all the days of my life. I ask You for this. I must have Him! I must have Him for me!"
>
> Then the Holy Ghost spoke, and I began to repeat after Him:

> What I really want to say is I would like to live where He lives. I implore You for this, my Father, above everything that I have asked for today. This I beg You from the very bottom of my heart. I would love to dwell in His house everyday of my life and to see His glory. I ask you to take me into the holy of holies where the Holy Ghost lives and let me live there with Him everyday and every night of my life. I want this so badly; I am begging you for it. Please let me live behind the veil with the Holy Ghost always and forever—like Samuel did as a boy sleeping next to the Ark of the Covenant and like David did as a man all the days of his life.

In saying these words to my Father, I found myself expressing the same innermost desires that David had in his heart so many years before. I felt privileged to be in such good company.

At that moment I realized that God had answered David's request in Psalm 27, even unto allowing him to bring the feared and respected Ark of the Covenant (or God's abode) into his household—something unheard of at that time. From that day onwards, God manifested Himself to David almost all of the time, living with him in his house. What I was requesting had one significant difference. I was not moving the Ark physically into my home but only the Inhabitant of the Ark, the Holy Ghost Himself. He was all I needed, and all I could request anyway because I did not know how to get the Ark for myself. It was immaterial anyway because unlike David, I was living in a time after Jesus died at Calvary and after the veil of the tabernacle was torn. So the Inhabitant of the Ark did not live there anymore, and it was He that was being sought after not the Ark itself. Whatever its location today; the Ark remains uninhabited.

I continued,

> Please also grant me permission to see the face and body of the Holy Ghost, to look upon His Glory just like David requested. David had all these glorious experiences with Your Manifest Presence, and I want them too. Since I will be living with Him in His house, please grant that we will forever be inseparable and that He will go with me wherever I go and I will go with Him wherever He goes. May Your people always know that He is with me. These things I really want. Finally, this is the cry of my heart. I know He calls Enoch His *best friend* but does He have room for one more? I would love to be His best friend too. He is all I want in this life. I am so lonely without Him, and my life has no purpose without Him. Please give Him to me. I promise that I'll take good care of Him and that I'll love Him.

With that said, I heard the Holy Ghost say, "Done. You shall have all that you ask for, and you shall dwell in the place you seek." With that it was over, and I just slumped onto the ground. Eventually, I used the rail to hoist my body up into the seat, and I went to sleep.

It might be quite a few years before God's promises come to pass in my life, yet I wait patiently year after year. Five years went by—then six, then seven, then ten years! Through it all, I have continued to believe God for His promises to me, for He is not a man that He should lie. (Numbers 23:19) These years of waiting are spent entertaining, worshiping and fellowshipping with the Manifest Presence of the Holy Ghost every night from midnight until three or four or even six or seven o'clock in the morning, and they are thoroughly enjoyed because He also waits with me. Anytime I begin to doubt the promises given to me by my Father at the crusade, the Holy Ghost reassures me that His promises will surely come to pass. "We must simply wait on Him," He says. "We must simply wait on Him" (Isaiah 40:31).

THE PRECIOUS HOLY GHOST

THE MORE TIME we spent together the more I learned about Him, how He functioned and operated, His personality and even His own unique character traits. I began to realize that God had His own way of doing things and that these ways were peculiar to Him. No one else on the planet did things the way He did them. As I spent more time with God, I began to see Him operate more and more in His ways; and as a result of this, I began to learn them.

God is a very comical character. He has a sense of humor out of this world. In fact He is the funniest person I know. This is no more evident than in the way He teaches His ways; because even to learn His ways, I had to learn them His way. To attempt to learn them any other way would result in a human interpretation and human perspective being superimposed on the reasoning and habits of a divine Person. This would result in terrible distortions in the minds of men of who God is, what His personality is really like, and how He actually behaves. In fact the truth about God would be replaced with how humans perceive Him, what they think His attitude towards things ought to be, and what His behavior should be like. So it is vital to learn God's ways, God's way.

The method He used to teach me His ways was first to orchestrate and expose me to a real life experience, and then afterwards He would show me a passage from the Bible that would explain His behavior. However, every time I pressed Him for an explanation as to why He would operate in a particular manner and for which there was no logical reason for doing so, He would answer me with two truly profound statements. First, He would proudly inform me that His thinking ability is far beyond logic. He thinks very differently from us humans. We would like to think that being made in His image means that we think like Him, but this is not so. Nothing could be further from the truth. It just means that we look like Him.

Secondly, there is His sovereign right to solve a problem in whatever manner He thinks fit. He simply explains it away by saying that it was one of His ways, it was His choice, and it was what He felt like doing at the time. This brought me to the tremendous realization of God's almighty omnipotence and supremely elevated position overlooking everyone and everything in the grand scheme of things. What I did not understand at first and what took a long time for me to grasp, is that He does things His way because they are His ways, He is God, and that settles it. He is free to do things or solve problems in His particular way simply because He is God and He is not at the mercy of anyone. He is not answerable to anyone to change His ways or to adopt anyone else's. Since He is God, it is up to me to learn His ways, not for Him to fall in line with mine. He is God after all, and if I had any respect for Him, I would adopt this attitude. So it is only fitting that the true servant would ask God to teach him His ways. The Holy Ghost is God too and just like the Father and the Son have ways that are peculiar to them, so also has He. Scripture says (Hebrews 3:7–11) that the Israelites saw God's wonders and the miracles performed by His hand, but did not know His ways. Only Moses knew His ways. I began learning God's ways in a very real way when I tried to quit smoking for the very first time after I got saved.

Before I came to know Jesus, I tried to stop smoking a few times, but I never succeeded because I found the stomach pains and the other symptoms which accompanied the withdrawal process far too overwhelming for me. As a result, I never got past the third day of the weaning–off process. However, after I experienced salvation, I decided to try my hand at quitting again for two reasons. The first was that I figured that I had God in my life now, and since He was on my side, I hoped that He would help me so that quitting would be different from before I was saved. I thought that perhaps God would do something so that it would be less painful an ordeal than my previous attempts.

Secondly, although I loved smoking, I was fed up with its ill effects. For some reason it caused me to suffer from memory loss, and it hampered my ability to concentrate fully, thus affecting my retention of information from both textbooks and lectures and affecting my studies on the whole. I noticed increased fertility in my brain matter and in my memory during the few occasions that I went without smoking. As a result, I attempted to quit smoking about three times after my salvation, but these attempts were also unsuccessful. I learned valuable lessons about God on each occasion, but I never managed to remain nicotine free for more than a few months, after which I resumed smoking all over again. I found it very frustrating because I felt that I had disappointed God, because the body is the temple of God and I felt I was defiling it with my smoking.

I carried this guilt around with me like a ton of bricks for a long time and did not lay it down; until one day the pastor of New Life Christian Fellowship

Church, seeing my disappointment, said to me, "If the Son would set you free, you will be free indeed." Immediately God touched his words with tremendous power. Out of the heavens power fell and traveled on the pastor's words from the moment they exited his mouth, just as he breathed them for me to hear. I was taken aback. I did not expect Jesus to speak. He gave no warning. What a wonderful surprise! The touch remained lingering on the words for a short while after they were said. This meant only one thing, that Jesus was speaking through the pastor. *It was good to hear God's point of view on the subject,* I thought, and at that moment I believed Him and laid down the ballast of guilt that I had been carrying around until now.

"What did He mean by these words?" I asked the Holy Ghost but received no reply. It would be another two years before my question would be answered, and I would experience and distinguish the vast difference between when a man does something in his human might to obtain moral standing before God, as opposed to God doing the job in the man—and for the man—without the man's help, so that all glory can then be given to God by the man. In 1999 when God told me that now was the time to stop smoking and took my addiction away painlessly and gently, I did not experience any of the effects of withdrawal, which I previously had to endure. No, not one of the many that I was forced to endure when I tried to quit on my own strength without getting a promise from God and His power. There was no pain, no hunger, no weight gain, no stomach cramps, and no desire to have a cigarette at all. In 1999 it took one day for God to completely deliver me of nicotine addiction and that was that; I have not smoked since and never will again. God made sure of that because my allergies, which were a constant source of irritation throughout my childhood (but which later went into a dormant phase during my ten years as a smoker) were miraculously revived, and now every time someone lights up a cigarette near to me, I begin to sneeze incessantly, and my eyes begin to run. Furthermore, I began to cough terribly when I was around smokers as I now found that secondhand smoke, which once had a pleasant aroma to me, now suffocated me and made me nauseous. Unbelievably I also found myself hating the stench of cigarettes and cigars. This was both the stale smell that pilfers through and attaches itself to the fibers of smokers' clothing, as well as the strong smell of a freshly–lit cigarette as its contents were being inhaled. Both scents made me nauseous and could induce vomiting if endured for prolonged periods of time. I could not believe what God had done. I could not return to cigarettes even if I wanted to. Truly he who the Son sets free is free indeed. This had come to pass and had become reality in my life.

However, this was not the case when I tried to quit smoking without Him and His words in 1998. In the latter it was my attempt to set myself free, and so I failed and remained a prisoner to my addiction, resuming smoking only within a matter of months. This was what I meant by learning God's ways and not confusing them with man's ways.

I have come to realize that man is very good at weaving his ways among God's ways and labeling them as God's ways. This was a vital lesson to me of doing things God's way and getting results. Without knowing what I was actually doing, I had activated the Gospel and got God to do it for me. I cried out to Him for help because I could not quit smoking on my own strength and I cried out to Him until He orally (God's *Rhema* or spoken Word) answered me. When He answered me He said, "If the Son would set you free, you will be free indeed." This was a promise to me that if the Son sets me free (as opposed to me setting myself free) of my addiction, I would never be a slave to it ever again.

When God speaks promises, we can hold Him to them because "He is not a man that He should lie nor the Son of man that He should change His mind" concerning the terms of the promise once they are laid out (Numbers 23:19). That means that it is impossible for the Father to lie or for Jesus to lie. It is not part of their divine nature to lie, so if Jesus tells you something, you can bet your last dollar it is going to happen. It must come to pass, and that is what the Bible emphasizes so much which I had missed out on so badly.

Throughout the centuries all the people in the Bible to whom the Father or Jesus gave promises, all of those promises have come to pass without exception. So I too could hold Him to His promise to me, and lo and behold, in 1999 God decided to perform the promise He gave me back in 1997 and set me free of my addiction. It was easy, painless, took no effort at all on my part, and had an everlasting effect. I will never have a relapse! Never! It is amazing that all I had to do was believe God. He did not do it at the time I wanted Him to, but instead He made me wait a year and asked me to quit at a very untimely time—two months before my Masters exams in law. This was all to see if I trusted Him enough and believed His words to me. This is faith, and it is impossible to please God without it. Had I learnt this before, I would have saved myself months and perhaps years of damage to my self-confidence and self-esteem, trying to do God's job for Him.

During one of my attempts to quit smoking on my own before God took my addiction away in 1999, the Holy Ghost started showing me some of His ways. I began to realize that each member of the Godhead has individual and separately characteristic ways to themselves. The Holy Ghost in particular—since He lives on the earth and not in Heaven—can take bodily form and has ways that are peculiar to Him. One of the Holy Ghost's ways is to make the three parts of the Godhead and the Bible very real and tangible experiences for me.

To achieve this, He taught me His ways by first making me experience them in a real yet supernatural way and then later showing them to me in the Bible. One of these experiences happened during one of those three instances when I tried to quit smoking without a promise from God or an oral command from Him, and so I resumed smoking a few months later. The experience was so shockingly real that it will remain with me forever, and it is this experience that I will share with you now.

Prior to God taking my addiction in June 1999, I had been a smoker for nine years and during all of that time not a day passed without my having a cigarette. I was a nicotine *addict* in every sense of the word from age twenty to twenty nine just prior to me completing my Masters degree in International and Commercial law and leaving university. I smoked an average of twelve cigarettes daily which increased to about sixteen or eighteen when I was in the midst of exams. I was fed up of smoking; so when I went home for my summer holidays in 1998, I tried to quit smoking because it was affecting my memory and concentration, which in turn was affecting my studies. Jesus did not ask me to stop smoking until just before I did my Masters exams in August 1999, so I was doing this purely for academic reasons.

So I asked all three persons of the Trinity especially the Holy Ghost to help me in my endeavor, and then I quit *cold turkey,* I abstained from having any cigarettes at all on the first day. It was the hardest thing I had ever done in my life. The withdrawal pains were so intense that I experienced severe stomach cramps. They were the closest thing to what I imagined a woman's period pains would have felt like. I also experienced sweating and shivering, and I was constantly agitated. I became so cold that I could feel it deep in the very marrow of my bones. I was also hungry all of the time and must have put on five pounds on the first day alone. Eventually the withdrawal pains became so overbearing that I had to cry out to Jesus to come in and put me out of my agony. Immediately I was put to sleep. I do not remember anything more about the first day except that it was a Saturday because the Lord just knocked me out cold and put me into a deep sleep. I awoke the next day very rested. I should have been—after all I had slept for almost twelve continuous hours from Saturday into Sunday!

The second day was almost as bad as the first, and so the Lord put me to sleep on that day also. In this painful state of nicotine deprivation, whenever I prayed or worshiped, especially at midnight, the Presence and the power of God were multiplied ten, maybe even twenty times its usual intensity. On these two days, the intimacy between God's Presence and me had increased to the point that it was overpowering. It was too much to handle. He would come very close to me—closer than ever before—and I would feel unworthy and not allow Him to come right up to me. I did not understand that He was trying to relieve me of my withdrawal pains and that I was preventing Him from doing so every time I pushed Him away.

On the third day I rose from my bed early, had breakfast, showered, and resolutely decided that I didn't care what people said about the body being the temple of God—I needed a cigarette, and I needed it now! My plan was to hop into my car, drive down to the nearest twenty–four hour service station and buy a pack of 555 cigarettes, which was my preferred brand at that time. Just as I was making up my mind to do this, my mother asked me to buy some things for her from the same service station. *It was all very convenient,* I thought. I apologized to the Father, to Jesus, and to the Holy Ghost for surrendering to my nicotine craving. I kept pleading with the Holy Ghost over and over, "Holy Ghost please forgive me, but this is the best that I can do. Please, my Friend, do not be disappointed with me." Then I picked up my car keys from the study and rushed outside to my car. It all happened so quickly. From the moment that I made up my mind to resume smoking and buy the cigarettes, there was a powerful and undeniable Presence standing behind me. I could feel His glory burning a hole in my back. However, my mind was not on Him; it was on one thing and one thing only—cigarettes. Anything to stop the pain my body was in. I was walking very swiftly and could almost taste the flavor of a cigarette in my mouth; I wanted one so badly. As I headed out of the house into the large garage, I felt that something or someone was following me. I could feel someone's body or Presence hot on my heels, running just two or three paces behind me, but I did not stop to acknowledge or investigate Him. However, the reality of someone nipping at my heels was unmistakable.

I occasionally felt the toes of His feet stepping on my heels and on my Achilles tendon as He swiftly followed me very closely, sometimes too closely, through the garage towards my car. I could even hear the slight pitter–patter of His swiftly moving feet. *Pitter! Patter! Pitter! Patter!* I ignored Him and increased my stride and my speed, leaving whoever was following me further and further behind. I was now far ahead of whoever was following me when my mother called out to me, "George!" She wanted to add a few things to the list. So I stopped suddenly in my tracks and very quickly turned 180 degrees to head back into the house, only to inadvertently come face to face with the Holy Ghost who had been following me, who did not stop running, but who was now coming right at me at full speed. I was immediately face to face with a very strong rushing Wind who hit me in the face and throughout the front of my body. My heart stopped as I beheld the awesome sight of this fast moving Wind in the shape of a man, Who ran right into me and collided with me with such tremendous force that there was no way I could withstand Him, and I was immediately knocked backward onto the ground, flattened, where I lay slain in the Holy Ghost.

I exclaimed loudly, "Oh God!" at the moment of collision. But He was running way too fast to stop, and that was it. We collided, and I was knocked backwards onto the ground. I could not believe what I had just seen. I saw His face and His whole body at the moment of impact and His image remains etched in my memory to this day. As this fierce Wind blew me over and the powerful force of this man in the Wind collided with me, the last thing I remember before hitting the ground was that there was joy everywhere. The Wind was full of it, and although I now lay on the ground, I was smiling and giggling at all the funny things Jesus was saying to me. I lay there for a few moments hearing Jesus speak crystal clearly to me and telling me how much He loved me, and that I was not to go to the service station today, but that I should leave it for another day when I would not be tempted to buy cigarettes. I could hear Him very clearly and very loudly. I had never heard Him speak so clearly before. The Holy Ghost also sang sweet songs to me very clearly, and I awoke from the slain state only to find the Manifest Presence of God sitting beside me on the ground waiting for me to awaken. I sat up, and there He was right next to me at ground level—sitting, waiting, singing.

I looked Him full in the face and said, "Hi."

He smiled, and said, "Hi. I was trying to get your attention to tell you not to go to the service station, but you were bent on going and you ignored me." I felt terrible for having ignored Him and treating Him this way, and I apologized profusely to Him. He immediately forgave me. I realized that I felt much better now. I had no craving for cigarettes. It left me when I ran into the Holy Ghost. At the moment of collision, something was dislodged in my belly that speedily rose up to my mouth, only to be forcefully expelled out of my body through my mouth as wind. The force behind the expulsion and removal of this wind was so powerful, that it contributed to the force that knocked me backwards onto the ground and flat onto the garage floor.

I did not try to get up from the ground because the most beautiful thing was happening. The Holy Ghost remained seated on the ground beside me, and I could feel His knees pressing against my ribcage. He was singing sweet praises to Jesus the Lamb of God and speaking to me at the same time. Each word that came out of His mouth was touched with joy. Each sentence He uttered had a fresh touch of joy on it. As He leaned over me speaking and singing to me, I could see a beautiful white light emanating from His form, which I know now was His *shekinah* glory. He was encircled with the most glorious hue and a joyful mist so thick that I could part it with my fingers. I felt very light-headed and was filled with joy, and I could not stop smiling. I felt as though someone had administered an anesthetic by placing one of those anesthesia masks over my face as they do in surgery, and I was inhaling the sweet smelling gas and falling into a deep and blissful sleep. I was totally at rest and at peace, and I did not want to get up. I did not want it to end. It was all too beautiful. It was the most beautiful and joyful experience I have ever had. I did not get up. I just laid there and enjoyed the peace. However throughout the whole experience, I had a nagging question in my mind, and before I could even ask the Holy Ghost the question, He answered it.

> Yea though I walk through the valley of the shadow of death I will fear no evil for Thou art with me, Thy rod and Thy staff they comfort me. Surely goodness and mercy shall *follow me* all the days of my life, and I shall dwell in the House of the Lord forever.
>
> Psalm 23: 6

I did not understand why He was relating this portion of Psalm 23:6 to me, but in my euphoric state, I could hear Him explain, "You were walking through a valley, and I will always be with you when you are walking through a valley both now and in times to come. It is my nature to be with people when they are walking through valleys. I would never leave them alone under such circumstances. I always walk *behind* them when going through valleys, not beside them and not ahead of them. That is why David the Psalmist wrote that I *followed* him through the valley. I can only *follow* someone if I am walking *behind* them. The reference to *goodness and mercy* is a reference to Me." I did not understand. So I asked Him what He meant, and He answered my question with questions:

"Who is good all the time and whose mercy endures forever?" He asked.

"God alone is good and His mercy endures forever." I responded.

"Well," He said, "*goodness and mercy* represent God. So if *goodness and mercy* shall follow me all the days of my life, it means that God shall follow me all the days of my life." It all made sense to me now. That is why I felt Him running behind me because He was *following* me through the valley and so when I stopped and turned around suddenly to run in the opposite direction, I found myself facing Him. He was still running and ran right into me.

Then realization hit me. He did it on purpose to relieve me of my withdrawal pains. He knew the agony I was in and how badly my body and mind were crying out for a cigarette, so He came to take my pain away. About twenty minutes later, I got up from the ground with the Holy Ghost still next to me telling me not to go to the convenience store today, but to leave it for another day when I would be better able to deal with the temptation of buying cigarettes. So I staggered back into the house and went to bed, drunk in the Holy Ghost, and still giggling with joy (See Joel 2:19, 24; Amos 9:13; and Acts 2:15–18). I slept right through the remainder of the afternoon through the night and into the morning of the next day.

Needless to say, my Mother wanted to know why I was not going to do the errand for her anymore. I explained the situation of the station selling cigarettes, and I was not ready to face that temptation, which she understood.

This was how I learned God's ways. He performed them first, walking me through the pages of the Bible in a very real and physical way, and then He would show me the experience in scripture and explain it to me.

The week before I quit smoking, I had been asked by the pastor of a new and upcoming Church called *The Living Room* to play a few songs on the guitar for worship at one of his cell group meetings the following Wednesday. I was delighted and honored to be asked to do it and without hesitation gave him an enthusiastic, "yes!" I had attended this cell group before, and it comprised of many young people, all of whom were excited and thirsty for more of God. The pastor asked me to play no more than three songs to God for the short worship period on my acoustic guitar to begin the cell group meeting. Well that was easy because there was actually only one song on God's heart and mind that week; it was called "How Lovely is Your Dwelling Place" by Matt Redman. I tried to find two other songs to play after it, but God did not care about any other song. He only wanted to hear that song. He absolutely loved it and could not get enough of it, so I played it over and over for Him that week. He never grew weary of it.

Every time I played it especially the arpeggio–filled introduction which I had composed for the beginning, God's Manifest Presence would just walk into my bedroom and lead me in singing it. He would touch different parts of the song at different times to show me specifically what was on His mind that day and what He was trying to say. Without a doubt this song was very special to Him at the time. The words of the song talked about living every day in the Presence of God and with the Presence of God, to have Him everywhere I go and doing everything with me. About having His Holy Ghost everywhere I went, and that life is not worth living unless He is there. It spoke of a deep hunger to have Him, His Presence, and not just His works or power in my life. It was from one of the worship books I used at the Christian Union.

Wednesday had arrived. It was the fifth day of my attempt to quit smoking, so I was still experiencing periodic cravings and stomach cramps. The time for the cell group meeting had arrived, and it was being held at one of the cell group member's home that was very close to my parents' house. We all sat in her living room, and after greetings and hugs were exchanged, we chatted until the pastor started the meeting. He then asked me to lead worship, so I picked up the guitar. While still seated, I began to play the song very slowly.

As the arpeggio part was being played, I could feel the atmosphere in the room changing. Little by little it became charged with electricity, and I could sense that something was about to happen. I pushed this thought from my mind and concentrated on singing to God and playing to Him. When all of a sudden, He manifested Himself appearing at the front door of the apartment, and He was looking right at me. I looked up and smiled at Him, and in a flurry of wind He made a beeline straight for me. I was sitting at the opposite end of the room from the door, so He had to run past everyone to get to me, which He did in a split second like a mighty gust of wind blowing past everyone, leaving behind in His wake some startled, shaken, weeping, and very surprised young people. Some of the people were physically knocked back into their seats. Some just started weeping, but most were in shock because nobody expected Him. No one expects God to come into a church or a cell group meeting even though the meeting is for Him. *How sad,* I thought. This was the first time He had ever moved and manifested Himself and made contact with the public as He went by. All the times before, the contact was just between Him and I alone. He ran past the pastor and knocked him back into his seat, and He ran past a few others before finally reaching me, then He wrapped His arms around me to remove my withdrawal pains again, sending the guitar flying across the room in the process.

I sat there weeping holding Him as He held me. I was locked in His embrace as He removed my withdrawal pains by merely making contact with me. I had been feeling them for about one hour before the meeting, and I tried to endure them. But they had become so unbearable that I was pleading with God to take them away. Well, He did. In a very physical and real way, He showed up to take my pain away from me personally. I felt like Shadrach, Meshach and Abednego to whom the Holy Ghost appeared in a very real and physical way to save them from death in the fiery furnace (Daniel 3:25). He is so wonderful! I felt so privileged that He would do this for me! His hug felt so wonderful that I did not want the moment to end. He passed on joy and peace and took away my pain. My withdrawal pains were now gone. It was instantaneous! I continued to let Him hug me because it was a very good hug. He always gives good hugs! I felt warm all over, happy, and filled with joy. I was oblivious to everyone else around me and focused on Him, thanking Him for coming to my rescue.

Then the pastor got up and collected the guitar which was now on the floor about two meters away from me and brought it back to me. At the same time, the Holy Ghost got up and lingered behind me. I looked around the room. It looked like a hurricane had blown through it. People's hair was tossed every which way, some were sobbing, some were smiling, some looked shocked and surprised, and everyone wanted to know and understand what had just happened. The pastor asked me to explain to everyone what had just taken place. They already knew that I had quit smoking just five days before, but what they did not know was that everyday I would experience the pain of withdrawal and everyday I would play this very same song to the Holy Ghost, and He would come to me and take my pain away. Today was just another one of those days.

So I began, "He really likes the song we were singing earlier. We have been playing it all week, and He shows up whenever I play it. So when He heard it, He came running to the front door and knowing the pain that I was in, He ran to me, wrapped His arms around me and took my pain away all at one go. Now I feel fine."

I looked at the faces of the people all around me. They did not know what to say. Some of them believed me, and some did not know what to believe. All that was known for sure was that someone or something ran into the building, past everyone, and made contact with everyone in an effort to get to me, because they all felt Him or were moved to tears by Him. So at the pastor's request, we resumed the song, and His Presence increased a little bit. However, this time it was not as intense as before because He had already accomplished what He came in to do. He came to rescue me.

. . . A RUSHING MIGHTY WIND

(Acts 2:2)

IT WAS MARCH 1999, and I was in the process of doing my Masters in International and Commercial Law at the University of Buckingham in Buckinghamshire, England. I had moved to the quieter and more picturesque living quarters of the Hunter Street Campus, which had a crystal clear river running through it called the river Ouse (Pronounced = ooze). It was home to a pair of majestic swans who glided gracefully across the water, and three of the noisiest and most presumptuous geese you could ever find. They arrived outside my window every morning and with a loud honking and frolicking demanded breakfast and attention. I named them Larry, Curly, and Mo. Mo was the only female, so I named her after Mo. It was a beautiful place to live, a picture perfect scene; something you would see on a postcard advertising the gorgeous English countryside or in a children's fairy tale book.

I moved into room forty five on the first floor of Hailsham House (named after Lord Hailsham of St. Marylebone, who was one of the chief supporters of the first private university in England, namely the University of Buckingham), which I easily settled into within a few days. The law faculty and the Franciscan law library were a ten minute walk uphill from the Hunter Street campus, and so I made this journey every time I had a lecture or whenever I needed to use the library, which was four days a week. The immediate surroundings of Hailsham House comprised of the business school library, the Masonic building, an administrative building called the Yeomanry House, the Old Town Mill (home to the student union), the university pub, and the refectory (that served sumptuous breakfasts and lunches to students daily). Christian Union meetings were held every Wednesday evening at 6:00 p.m. in the Masonic building, above a room reserved for Masonic meetings which were held on other evenings.

Every Wednesday evening at about 5:30 p.m., I lugged my guitar and my very heavy amplifier across from my room in Hailsham House over to the Masonic building to set up my equipment and to lead worship at 6:00 p.m., which was a journey of about only two minutes but took nearly ten minutes because of the weight of the amplifier. I thanked God for moving me from Verney Park campus to Hunter Street, because to lift my cumbersome amp from the former to the Masonic building and back again every Wednesday would have required great strength, stamina, and a taxi every time.

For the duration of two years (1998 and 1999), I was the worship leader of the Christian Union on campus and led—well actually the Holy Ghost led—the Christian Union meetings in worship every Wednesday. I would set up my electric guitar and amplifier and play the three songs that God had touched for that week. He always chose three songs. In early 1998 just before I became worship leader, my midnight date with God went through some changes. I no longer worshiped with the walkman and sang along; now I was playing my guitar and worshiping Jesus *live.* However, God's *modus operandi* remained the same. The Holy Ghost would arrive promptly at midnight and lead me in worship. I had always wanted to learn how to play the guitar, and the Holy Ghost taught me in a very real and physical way. But that is another story. I now worshiped using Spring Harvest worship books that were teeming with songs and that were used by the New Life Christian Fellowship Church's worship team, of which I had also become a member. So I worshiped God with the songs we played in church every Sunday.

Every week I would rummage through the book and find songs that He *liked.* By *like,* I mean if the song spoke about the issues that were on His heart that week or what was on His mind, then He would touch the song with tremendous power and enter my room and fill it with Himself the moment I strummed the first few chords. For the two years that I was worship leader of the Christian Union, I played the three songs that were on God's heart and mind for that week and no others. Every week that was all I did, and reliably every week for two years, God's Glory and Presence filled the room where the Christian Union meeting was held. People asked me how I did it so consistently. It was simple. Give God what He wants, and He will come. Play the songs He is singing and what He wants you to play not the songs you want to play, and He will come. Play the songs He *likes* or His *favorite* ones at the time, not your own, and He will come. The songs that God touched with power were the songs that He *liked* or were His *favorites* at the time. All I had to do was to find out which three songs He touched with power. So I would worship Him at midnight with my guitar and discover which three songs they were; during which, He would walk into my room and fill it with Himself. There was always one song which was much more touched than all the others. It was usually a slow intimate love song to God, and it was always played last at the Christian Union meeting, to give Him enough time to fill the room with Himself and to minister to the members. He would not leave until they were full and satisfied with an overflowing abundance of His unforgettable Presence.

One Wednesday evening a little before 6 p.m., I was setting up my amplifier and guitar at the front of the room where the Christian Union met and was chatting with the pastor and an elder of the New Life Christian Fellowship Church. The Church had started the Union many years before, and these men—sometimes accompanied by the senior pastor—always attended the meetings, which they thoroughly enjoyed. They were very young at heart, loved young people, and always found the diverse cultures of the university's youth very exciting and interesting. In walked a stranger through the back door, who smiled as he approached us and asked if this was the venue for the Christian Union meeting and if it was open for anyone to attend. He received a hearty welcome from the pastor who assured him that anyone could be a part of it. The pastor introduced himself and stretched forth his hand to shake the stranger's hand. The stranger took his hand in his own and then the elder's hand and introduced himself as Ramón Raveneau from St. Lucia. I overheard this part of the conversation and was pleased to find another person from the Caribbean in Buckingham, especially from St. Lucia which is only a twenty minute flight off the northwest coast of Barbados. I had now completed setting up my equipment, and the students had ceased filing into the meeting room. There were about twenty–five students present that day.

I stood at the front of the room facing everyone and began to pray, basically the same prayer I uttered at every meeting, with slight variations of it every week, "Precious Jesus, we come to worship You and our Father today, and we humbly ask that Your Presence will be made manifest in this place and be among us in a very real and intimate way." Then I would whisper an invitation for only the Holy Ghost to hear, "Please come my Friend and lead this worship. I cannot do it without You. I need You now. Please come and be with me. I do not know how to worship without You. Tell me what to do moment by moment, song after song, and line after line. I will follow Your every move, and I now completely surrender to Your leading, my Gentle Friend. Please come." Within seconds an electric charge could be felt in the atmosphere, and His glory would begin to fill the room little by little even before I had strummed the first chord. I immediately thanked Him for coming and beckoned Him to give us even more of Himself. Second only to my private intimate worship alone with God, I loved leading a group of believers in worship because God's intense, exciting, and powerful anointing would fall from the heavens above, through the ceiling and alight upon my shoulders, weighing me down. The unbelievable joy and exhilaration that came with it was a feeling just too exciting and awesome for words to describe. Any person in ministry will testify to that, but I was not in ministry; or was I? I thought I was just a university student, but others believed differently.

I always played the fast worship songs that were on God's heart that week first and the slow love songs for intimate worship afterwards. The Holy Ghost gave me this recipe the night before I led my very first Christian Union meeting worship session. He said it was called praise and worship in that order because the fast songs of praise were sung to God first, and then the slower songs for worship were sung to Him afterwards. He showed me the reason for this from (Psalm 100:4) that praise is only used to *enter* into God's gates, but if I wanted to approach God closely to touch and embrace Him or even sit upon His lap and listen to Him, this will require worship. So during the praise segment, students sang, clapped, and danced to the fast songs. Then the Holy Ghost said,

"Sing it again from the top." Without missing a beat, I started singing the song all over again, and then He touched the chorus. I sang the chorus again, and He touched it again. So I sang it another time. Then He touched one line in the chorus. So I sang that line, and He touched it again and again. As He did so, I sang it until He no longer touched it. With each time I obeyed

His leading to sing something over and over, His Presence in the place grew progressively thicker until He filled it.

Just as we ended the song and the others had stopped singing, His Presence was still traveling on the music as I played slow, gentle arpeggios on my guitar. Suddenly there was this exuberance and loud clapping and the exclamation of, "Bravo! Bravo! Well done!" It was Ramón. He was beside himself with the experience of God's Presence, and the steadily deepening anointing traveling on the music especially the guitar playing. He sat down, thinking the worship was over and received many cold stares from some of the other students for his outburst. Others just snickered. I know I did. He did not realize how seriously and soberly the others took worship. How I wish we were all free to react to worship as freely as he did! We followed the Holy Ghost into the second song of praise, and Ramón sheepishly stood up again to rejoin the praise. At this point, I wanted so much to burst into laughter, but just then God's physical Presence walked into the meeting and directed us as to what line was touched and what song to sing again, at the same time filling the room with more and more of Himself until the faster songs of praise were over. Then we moved into the slower and more intimate song where we worshiped Him and sang and whispered sweet words of love to Him. To me that was as close to Jesus' heavenly throne room worship with the angels and elders that we saints can get on this earth. However, I believe we can always have the intimacy and awesomeness of Jesus' throne room worship if we just ask Him for it and follow Him. During the worship, the Holy Ghost was very touched by the words of the love song we were singing to the Son, to the Father, and to Him. So He moved around the room touching and ministering to each worshiper there. I looked up from my guitar and saw His Manifest Presence moving from and ministering to one individual after another. It was easy to follow Him around the room because each person He was standing before would quietly shed tears, simply because it is nearly impossible to stand in such close proximity to the Manifest Presence of God and not cry. (I was surprised they could even stand in His Presence. The usual reaction to Him is that people buckle under their weight and fall flat on the floor.) When He had ministered to most of the people in the room, I began to play softer and slower, but He was enjoying their worship so much that He really did not want to leave. So I continued playing slow arpeggios to the chords of the song until He had His fill, and then worship ended.

I have never just put down the guitar, ignored God who was still standing in the room, and begun the scripture reading or went on with the planned activities. That would just be down-right rude, discourteous, and selfish of me. Having worked so hard to get

God's Manifest Presence in the room, it was now time to thank Him for coming, and to chat with Him to make Him feel welcome, and to find out what was on His mind that day, and whether anything was bothering Him. I did these things when I was alone with God in my room but not at Christian Union meetings for fear that someone would think that I was out of my mind. At Christian Union meetings, the most I could do was thank Him for showing up and tell Him that I loved Him. He was enjoying Himself so much that He lingered around the room for quite a while before letting the worship cease. I thanked Him for coming and invited the whole group to do the same, which they did. Minutes later someone shared a message that God had placed on their heart, which they first read from the Bible and then explained what the Lord had revealed to them. The meeting was a lot of fun; one I would not forget.

At the end of the meeting as I was packing up my equipment, Ramón came over to me and asked, "So are you from India?"

"No." I responded.

"Well then you must be from Pakistan." He tried again persistently.

"No, I am from Barbados." I replied, putting an end to his guessing game.

"Really! I am from St. Lucia just around the corner from your island."

"Yes I know. I heard you tell the pastor earlier." I responded.

"You play that guitar really well. You should play professionally." I smiled and thanked him for his compliment. Then he got serious and apologized for his loud but appreciative outburst, "I have never heard worship like that before. I thought it was really good!" I realized that he was being very honest with me, and I appreciated it and thanked him. He offered to carry my amp across to my room for me, which he did, and we chatted along the way. He had a slight stammer which became progressively less the more he talked.

He spoke about what things were like back home, and he told me he had family in Barbados, whom he visited from time to time. It turns out that we both liked Accra Beach and Sandy Beach. They were both our favorite beaches on my island. I had visited St. Lucia when I was in my teens and remembered it as a very pretty and unspoiled island. He filled me in on recent events in St. Lucia until we arrived at my door, and after he carried my amp inside, we said goodbye. We would have chatted longer if I did not have a study group meeting to attend.

On Thursday night or actually early Friday morning at 2:30 a.m., I was hard at work researching and writing an essay due for submission later that day. When suddenly, out of nowhere, the Holy Ghost spoke and instructed me to go downstairs. I was deeply engrossed in my essay and did not want to leave it at the time, but I obeyed Him, grabbed a sweater, and headed downstairs. I was immediately obedient to God. If you had asked me why I was closing my window, locking my door, and heading downstairs, I would have told you that I did not know. All I knew was that the Holy Ghost had just appeared for a brief moment, not even for a full three seconds and had commanded me to do this. He had done this a few times before, and each time I obeyed. However, this time I was a little worried because I was nowhere near to finishing my essay, and it was getting late. I knew that I would soon fall asleep, and before this happened I wanted to complete my assignment. Meanwhile, God seemed oblivious to my deadline, and now He was adding something else for me to do. Regardless, I obeyed Him.

It was March, and although it was a very cold winter's night, I still stepped outside in my short pants. I had developed a reputation among my neighbors for wearing short pants outdoors in the heart of winter. I had the island mentality of wearing *baggies* (surfer's shorts) to go anywhere in Buckingham much to the embarrassment of my friends. I just could not change my *native* programming no matter how hard I tried, and so I gave up trying. Tonight would be no different. I would head out into the cold winter's night in immediate obedience to God at 2:30 a.m., clad in nothing more than a sweater and shorts. I went downstairs, walked through the communal kitchen, and exited the building, allowing the door to slam shut and lock behind me. God's wish was my command, and I followed His request.

As I smelled the fresh night air and watched clumps of snow dissolve into the grass, who should I see turn the corner and saunter down the pathway towards me, but Ramón. *What are the chances of this?* I thought. *Did the Holy Ghost set up a chance rendezvous?* My mind flashed back to all of the times He had done this in the past when He would tell me to go somewhere immediately, and the person at the rendezvous point was always alone and ready to experience salvation. Almost fifty three people had received salvation in this manner within the last two years, yet I was only a two–year–old Christian ushering them into the Kingdom of Heaven with most of the individuals experiencing an outpouring of power, baptism in the Holy Ghost or some other miraculous phenomenon as evidence of God's power.

I watched him approach and stand in front of me, laughing at me wearing shorts outdoors in the freezing cold. I was smiling too, brimming over with the full confidence of knowing that God was setting him up and that He lay behind the scenes orchestrating everything that was now taking place and was yet to take place within the next few minutes. I could not help myself from exuding this confidence as I spoke, mainly because I could feel the glory emanating from the Holy

Ghost who now stood very closely behind me. His Glory was so strong and concentrated, emitting powerful rays like the sun, that I felt that it could burn a hole in my back and scorch all the hair and skin on the back of my neck and legs. He began to speak, and I repeated everything He said. "So are you ready to talk?" I started in mid conversation as if Ramón and I had been chatting before. It left him hanging in mid–air.

"Talk about what?" he asked.

"Those hundreds of questions you have about God," I continued, repeating everything the Holy Ghost told me to say.

"How do you know about them?" he asked.

We went into his room which just happened to be my old room from the semester before (Room 34 Hailsham House), and we talked until about four thirty that morning about God and the questions which he had about things that happened in the Bible. Ramón then shared with me that when he found out he was going to Buckingham to study for two years and was going to be away from home; he made a decision that he was going to use this time to study and to get closer to God. How he was going to do this he was not sure. He told me that the day of the Christian Union meeting, he was walking through the law building around midday when he saw a poster advertising the meeting that evening, and he immediately felt a strong inexplicable urge to attend. He had given his life to Jesus at the tender age of seventeen or eighteen, and when I heard this, I asked the Holy Ghost why He had sent me to talk to Ramón when he was already saved. Right after I asked Him, the conversation turned to the topic of the Holy Ghost, about who He was and how He functioned. All the textbook questions were discussed. However, when I began telling him that I was not lonely on campus because the Person of the Holy Ghost keeps my company all of the time, he became very interested. I shared with him how He appears to me and leads me in worship every midnight in my room after which He hangs out with me, talking into the wee hours of the morning and how He recently began accompanying me wherever I went during the day even to all of my lectures. He would walk beside me, talk to me, and even sit beside me in lectures if there was a vacant seat next to mine. I could see that Ramón wanted the Holy Ghost as a living reality in his life too and to have experiences with Him much like I did. He also needed someone to answer the barrage of questions he had about God. He had compiled an endless list of questions over a period of years, some of them very personal to God and some very technical. It would take a man many months to answer them, and so it would be better for God the Holy Ghost Himself to personally give him the answers and explanations he needed. He asked me how to get Him in his life, and on the prompting of the Holy Ghost, I told him to ask God the Father for the

Holy Ghost and then to invite the Person of the Holy Ghost everyday into his prayer time or into his room a few times a day. With that said I left the room, headed for mine, finished my assignment, and went to bed.

Ramón and I quickly became good friends, but more importantly and much to my surprise, he was quickly becoming good friends with someone else—God! I should have realized how seriously he took our conversation that morning; when within only a few days, he began to exhibit the uncanny ability to tell where the Holy Ghost was standing after He entered my room. Ramón also got to know me quite well, well enough to tell when God was speaking to me. In about eight weeks, I was even more shocked to discover that Ramón entertained God's Manifest Presence in his room much like I did in mine. The Holy Ghost began manifesting Himself in his room so that every time I went to visit Ramón I was surprised to find that he already had a Visitor. I would have just left the Holy Ghost in my room and gone over to Ramón's room to borrow something or just to pay him a visit, and there He would be in Ramón's room too. How grateful I was that He is omnipresent and could be in many places at once! He would be sitting on Ramón's bed, and they would be talking; or He would just be keeping his company in silence as Ramón studied. Then the Holy Ghost began to accompany Ramón to all of his lectures. I marveled as this young man began to taste what I had been experiencing for almost two years now. He stopped asking me the many questions he had on the Father, Jesus, Heaven, and the Bible; and instead, he turned to the Holy Ghost for answers Who sometimes gave him the most unexpected and surprising explanations he could ever imagine, explaining each from the Bible.

I was very proud of Ramón who later became president of the Christian Union after I graduated from Buckingham. He became a close personal friend of the Holy Ghost, Who frequently and sincerely expressed many times how much He loved Ramón. This bond of friendship and love between the two would soon be demonstrated for others to see and experience with dramatic and unforgettable results.

• • •

I MET RAMÓN in March 1999, and a few months later, Jesus had asked him to be baptized. Within a day or two he had made up his mind to be baptized, and he told the pastor of his decision. The pastor and other members of New Life Christian Fellowship organized the event. It was scheduled to be on the 29th August 1999, which was a significant day not only because it was the pastor's birthday (the pastor who would be immersing Ramón into the water), but also because it was one day before my last exam for my Masters in International and Commercial Law. So I decided that I was not going to attend but instead would make maximum use of the day to study for the exam. Ramón was not pleased with my decision. In fact he was very upset that I would miss his baptism albeit for a good reason. I was torn and asked the Lord what to do. He told me to study before and after the service and to use the service as a break from my studies. It would give my mind a good rest before resuming study in the evening. So I made up my mind to go to the baptism.

As the days went by, Ramón became increasingly excited and harbored an expectancy that some amazing and unforgettable experience was about to befall him. The day quickly arrived, and I was studying in my room early that morning when Ramón knocked on my door. I let him in, and he showed me all of the gifts he had received for his baptism from his friends at the Christian Union. He was very popular in the Union. I did not know what baptismal gift to give him. I had racked my brain and asked Jesus over the last couple of days and all He told me was to leave it to Him as He had a gift for Ramón. When Ramón entered my room, so did the Holy Ghost. I heard Jesus speak very clearly, and I relayed everything He told me to say to Ramón. Jesus said, "From this day forward, I give you My Presence, the Holy Ghost. He shall be with you all of the time. He will never leave you nor forsake you, and He will love you. This is my baptismal gift to you." Ramón received the Word with tears in his eyes and gratitude in his heart. From that day onward, the Holy Ghost accompanied Ramón wherever he went. I witnessed the phenomenon many times. They were never apart. Many times I felt the Holy Ghost's Presence long before I got a glimpse of Ramón coming around a corner. Ramón reminded me that the service commenced at three o'clock in the afternoon and asked me not to be late.

• • •

ONE HOUR BEFORE the service, I hopped into a car with some friends from New Life Christian Fellowship Church and headed down to a Baptist church in Winslow where the baptism was taking place. There were quite a few people at Ramón's baptism. Almost the whole congregation from New Life Christian Fellowship Church and almost all of the members of the Christian Union attended. Ramón and I had the same Christian counselor as young Christian men. She was a nurse who worked with the university and who tried to treat me when I had my depression before I was saved and miraculously healed. She continued to counsel me for a few weeks after my healing to ensure that as a newly–born babe in Christ I was properly nurtured and raised to love and fellowship with Jesus. She was very dear to me and to Ramón who also saw her from time to time as a Christian counselor when he first left St. Lucia and came to Buckingham to study. She sat at the back of the church while I sat somewhere in the middle with fellow students and most of the elders of New Life Christian Fellowship Church.

It was a quaint little church with low pews and a dainty little altar. It was very cute as if designed for lilliputians and had a matching fairy tale color scheme. It was chosen because it was the closest church to the university with a baptistery. The latter was located just in front of the altar, and it was small like a plunge pool for one, but sufficient to get the job done.

Ramón was to be baptized in the same manner as Jesus with his body completely submerged in water and brought out again, symbolizing the washing away of all of his sins. The pastor of New Life Christian Fellowship Church would lead the service, and both he and an elder would dip Ramón under the water to baptize him. The service began by them both reading portions of scripture, but nothing happened until Ramón appeared dressed in a large blue shirt. He smiled sheepishly at everyone and shared with the congregation why he wanted to be baptized. Instantly, the Holy Ghost began to trickle into the church. Little by little, He entered the building so slowly that it almost took place unnoticed. However, I noticed and so did some of the girls who began to cry as His Presence grew. Gradually God's glory occupied the church in the form of a dense mist or cloud, and there was joy everywhere. I looked all around the church's interior and could not believe what I was seeing. His

Presence was everywhere and getting thicker with each passing minute. Other members of the congregation had begun to cry as God's Presence intensified. I was busy watching God accumulate in the church and so missed what Scriptures Ramón read. Then immediately afterwards Ramón made his way into the baptistery with the pastor and an elder following close behind him. As this was happening, the Presence of God disintegrated into the atmosphere, and His Glory was gone. As I watched the two men wading into the baptistery, I could not believe what I was seeing—the Holy Ghost's Manifest Presence was in the water standing right behind Ramón, and power was radiating from Him towards the congregation. It was easy to detect the source from which the power emanated. The Holy Ghost was in the water, and He remained there taking the similitude or form of a man until Ramón was immersed and raised up out of the water. There was tremendous applause throughout the church, and Ramón and the two men made their way out of the baptistery by a gentle flight of steps. Instantly the Holy Ghost left the pool and took to the air in the form of a great gust of Wind. Without warning, He blew through the church from the congregation's right hand side to our left hand side with such tremendous force and such amazing speed that He was akin to a hurricane force wind. With that done, He proceeded to blow in the opposite direction with the same magnitude of force and the same velocity as a rushing mighty wind.

We were experiencing exactly what had happened at Pentecost in the Upper Room (with the exception of the visible descent of tongues of fire), and I could not believe my eyes. With each swift movement of the Wind from one side of the church to another, the congregation burst into weeping and cries of indescribable joy. Most of the congregation burst into tongues while others just stood or sat watching what was taking place, completely awestruck. All manner of languages could be heard. It was beautiful! This continued for quite a while. The Holy Ghost continued to blow around the church at great speed, and then He settled down in the back of the church next to where my counselor was standing. (By this time most people were standing.) Immediately she spoke fearlessly and succinctly, "I love you Ramón. I love you Ramón. The same way in which I used George to bring you to Me so also shall I use you." As God spoke this through our counselor, the whole congregation burst into tears especially the women. There was not a dry eye or face in the building. The entire church wept; everyone was overcome with emotion as God's Presence was so real and alive that day. Then just as mysteriously as the Holy Ghost had appeared—with one quick gust of Wind—He was gone.

What a baptism! Pentecost at a baptism! This was unheard of, but it had just happened. I was there and witnessed it all. I had always been taught that what happened in the Upper Room at Pentecost could never happen again. The reason I was given and have heard time and time again is that Pentecost was when the Holy Ghost first came to the Earth in the form of a rushing mighty Wind and was placed inside believers for the very first time. Today I know better. I asked Jesus why does the Holy Ghost come in like a rushing mighty Wind, and He instructed me to look at all of the instances where the Holy Ghost exhibited this type of behavior. So I did just that.

I examined the occasions where the Holy Ghost exhibited similar behavior and found that two conditions were present every time the Holy Ghost behaved in this manner. First, a person who has an intimate and physically personal relationship with the Holy Ghost and knows Him well as a Friend or Lover, having Him as an integral and completely necessary part of his life is the first requirement. Secondly, the Holy Ghost must be happy and overjoyed with the person who has the intimate relationship with Him. His happiness is on account of the person's obedience to do what God has told him to do. In Ramón's case, he obeyed Jesus telling him to be baptized and was in the process of doing so when the Wind came in. In the case of my leading worship at the cell group meeting, while I was suffering from nicotine withdrawal pains, there also I was obedient to God in leading worship at the meeting even though I did not feel up to it. Also when I was late for my date with God and arrived at half past midnight, opening my dorm door to commence worshiping the Father and the Son, the Holy Ghost rushed at me with vibrant enthusiasm to see me, bowling me over and knocking me to the ground. He was happy to see me obey the Father and keep my date with Him that He had instructed me to do a year and a half earlier and which I had been faithful to do every midnight for that period. Examining all of this has made me realize a character trait of the Holy Ghost; His coming in like a rushing Wind is how He expresses His joy to the person who has Him in his life and whom He holds very dear. It is how He expresses His love and joy to those He loves. I have also come to realize that the reason that experiences like Pentecost do not happen as often as they should is because man has not taken the time to get to know this Rushing Mighty Wind intimately. The Holy Ghost does not come rushing in all excited and happy to embrace a man who is practically a stranger to Him. He is reluctant to approach such men although that man lives a life of perfect faith, always obeying what the Father and Son tell him to do.

There is however an exception to these requirements to have Pentecost. As with anything in Christianity, God is not an ogre, and His rewards cannot be reduced merely to satisfying requirements and obedience. God has a heart and as such will lay aside His requirements for any believer who spends regular hours of intimacy with Him and who finds himself in trouble, crying out for help and moving His heart. Throughout history when God's heart has been moved with compassion for the man or woman whom He loves, He has been known to come in like the Rushing Mighty Wind that He is, to save that person from their predicament. Who would think that the Rushing Mighty Wind would have a heart and come rushing in to aid those whom the Wind loves? Except for intimacy, God will do away with all requirements, premises, and conditions necessary and will come in with hurricane force winds to rescue the one that He loves and knows intimately.

EXPERIENCES WITH THE HOLY GHOST

ONE SUMMER VACATION when I was home in Barbados from university, I was invited to visit a church called Courts of Praise in the parish of St. Joseph. I had never heard of the church before, but the Holy Ghost was excited about our visit. It was a fairly new church in that its members were young Christians, and the building was still under construction. It comprised of two stories—the ground floor which was cemented and fairly comfortable with plastic chairs arranged in rows and a portable podium placed at the front, while in contrast the floor above it needed a lot of work. The church services were supposed to be held on the first floor, but as it was not yet ready, they were being held on the ground floor.

By the time I arrived and entered the ground floor, worship had already begun. The saints were raising their voices in praise to God, and His Presence could immediately be felt. Song after song, they built the anointing, and His Presence grew in intensity and thickness. Then the congregation began to worship Jesus and the Presence of the Holy Ghost grew even thicker like a mist hovering over and amongst the people. The worship lasted for about one hour, and when it was over, the first floor was filled with His Presence. The pastor thanked the Holy Ghost for being there that morning and proceeded to share his message. That also took about an hour, and then he brought the service to a close. The pastor came over to me, introduced himself, and offered to show me around. He showed me the work that was completed as well as what still remained to be done on the ground floor, and then we began to climb a flight of stairs that led to a platform on the first floor directly overhead where we were just worshiping. The staircase was a temporary wooden structure with a feeble and wobbly handrail. The pastor walked up the staircase ahead of me, and I followed gingerly behind him picking my way up the stairs while trying not to put any of my weight onto the handrail. Five or six steps up the staircase, I began to feel God's Presence and His Glory being emitted from somewhere on the platform that was on my right hand side. I climbed another step, and the emission of His Presence and power became even more intense. By now I had no choice but to lean on the handrail as His power was far too strong for me. I climbed yet another step and looked over to my right, and there He was sitting right on the floor of the platform with His legs crossed as though He wanted to be as close to us as He possibly could while we were worshiping on the floor below. I peered through the emissions of His intense Presence to see His Manifest Presence pick Himself up from the semi-concreted platform floor, dust Himself off, look right at me, and smile. Now I was holding onto the handrail for dear life. Any sudden movements and His Presence would have bowled me over and down the staircase onto the concrete floor below. So I held on even tighter. He just stood there looking at me and me at Him. I was speechless. I wanted to tell the pastor Who I was seeing but could not bring myself to do so for fear of making a sound and losing His Manifest Presence. As we stood there staring at each other, the Holy Ghost said to me, "The Lord inhabits the praises of His people." Within a few seconds, He began walking away from us until He vanished out of sight before my very eyes. I was left standing alone with my jaw dropped. I was taken aback and took a little time to catch myself and to digest what I had just witnessed and heard. *What did He mean by what He said?* I wondered.

When we exited the building, I did not share my experience with the pastor because I was anxious to be alone with the Holy Ghost to ask Him the meaning of His statement. So I bid the pastor and his wife goodbye and headed home.

Later that night at midnight, I worshiped, and when the Holy Ghost walked into my room, I asked Him what He meant by "The Lord inhabits the praises of His people."

He replied, "Whenever the bride of Christ worships the Father and Jesus, I will come and abide among them." Then He proceeded to show me the scripture in Psalm 22:3.

This was the manner in which the Holy Ghost taught me God's ways and the Bible. He first walked me through a very real physical experience where I lived through and experienced for myself the actual occurrence of the event, and then afterwards, He would show me the scripture in the Bible and explain it to me. He has never taught me the other way around and continues to do so even today.

• • •

ANOTHER EXPERIENCE OCCURRED when I was a baby Christian and had just been saved. After worshiping one midnight in my dorm for three to four hours like I did every night, I said goodnight to the Holy Ghost and blew Him a kiss as He left my room. He effortlessly walked through the door, leaving me to get some sleep, and I climbed under the covers to drift off into deep slumber. I slept soundly for about an hour when I was rudely awakened by a very large presence in my room standing at the foot of my bed. It came in uninvited, and fear and dread filled my room. This very tall and wide satanic being had walked through my door and posted itself at the foot of my bed uncomfortably close to my feet. My room was filled with fear and darkness. All of the joy and power that filled my room only an hour before was now gone. I was petrified and did not know what to do. I froze under my sheets. I knew I was not in the Presence of my Friend the Holy Ghost because there was no joy or peace anywhere. "[I]n thy presence is fullness of joy" (Psalm 16:11). It was quite the opposite in fact. I feared for my well being.

Unsure as to what to do, I closed my eyes and whispered aloud asking the Holy Ghost to come and help me. Immediately, I heard a soft song being sung in my spirit, and as I began to sing it softly, suddenly there was an almighty sharp burst of power and an explosion of joy as the Holy Ghost came rushing into my room to rescue me. He darted through my dorm door like a flash of lightning and charged at the demon at the foot of my bed. Immediately, the demon took flight. Right then, I pulled the covers up over my head listening intently to what was going on and waiting for it to be over. The Holy Ghost chased it around the room and then out through the door. In a few seconds, it was over.

The enemy fled leaving the Holy Ghost and me alone. He did not even put up a fight. I lifted off my covers to find my room filled with the familiar thick Presence and joy of my friend once again. I was elated. I was so relieved that He heard my cry. I thanked Him for coming to my rescue to which He replied; "When the enemy shall come in like a flood, the Spirit of the Lord shall lift up a standard against him" (Is 59:19). Needless to say, I got out of bed and sat around with Him chatting well into the early hours of the morning. Once again, I had witnessed and experienced God's behavior first and was shown the scripture afterwards ... and once again He came in to rescue me.

• • •

ON A FEW occasions, I fell asleep on my bed or at my desk, and as the midnight hour approached, I could hear someone knocking at my dorm door or outside my window. The times I awoke to the knocking I found that it was just minutes to midnight and that it was time for my date with the Holy Ghost. So I would get up and start worshiping. At midnight the Holy Ghost would appear and lead me in worship, and I would follow Him. However, there were times when I was just too tired to get out of bed, and so I would roll over and resume my slumber. Every time that I tried this; the knocking would persist until I got out of bed and worshiped. I was always amazed at how real the knocking was. It sounded exactly like human knuckles rapping on my door. I had my suspicions that it was the Holy Ghost trying to wake me up to spend time with Him and to worship because the knocking always began around five minutes to midnight. It was never at any other time of the day or night. There were also a few occasions when I could hear footsteps running outside of my room as though someone wanted to be invited in. This running would go on until I woke up to worship. I did not know what to make of these experiences. I had never heard of anyone having similar experiences with the Holy Ghost, and I did not open the door to see who was knocking until almost seven months after the knocking started.

On that fateful night, I fell asleep on my bed, and I heard the familiar sound of someone knocking at my door. I awoke and looked at my alarm clock. It was five minutes to midnight, and I got up and opened the door. To my surprise, there He was standing in my doorway in all of His Glory, and He entered my room with His long train following thickly and richly behind Him, filling my room with each step. He entered grandly as a king would in all of His regal splendor. I stood to the side well out of His way as He made His majestic entrance into my room, and His royal train just kept on coming and coming until it completely filled my room. Now I knew Who was behind the door all along.

It took about five whole minutes for all of His train to enter, and when it was all there, there was nowhere available to stand. He occupied every molecule of the air in the room. *What an entrance,* I thought. As He stood there in all of His splendor, I stood in awe for about five minutes speechless at the sight that I now beheld. Tears gushed down my cheeks as there was so much of Him present.

Joy filled my room, and after a while I whispered to Him ever so softly, (it would have been discourteous to speak aloud in so much of His Presence) "Why were You knocking?"

To which He responded, "I sleep, but my heart waketh: it is the voice of my beloved that knocketh, saying, Open to me, my love, my dove, my undefiled," and then He continued, "Behold, I stand at the door, and knock: if any man hear my voice, and open the door, I will come in to him, and will sup with him, and he with me." An entire month would pass before I would find that His words were from the Song of Solomon 5:2 and Revelation 3:20 respectively.

Time and time again, God taught me in this manner and to this day He continues to do the same. He insists that I experience the event as a reality in my life first, and then He gives me the scripture and the explanation afterwards. The words in the Bible must come alive in my life first and actually happen, after all they are God's living Words; then the explanation is given afterwards.

IN HIS MANIFEST PRESENCE

AFTER YEARS OF face to face fellowshipping with the Holy Ghost, I have come to realize that the main purpose of Christianity and salvation is to restore us to the state of complete, uninhibited, and intimate fellowship with God which Adam had in the Garden of Eden before he fell and was separated from God by sin. God the Father asked Jesus to purchase us back from satan so that we could be like little Adams again having a physical relationship with an invisible God. Where we could go for walks with Him hand in hand in the cool evening sunset and talk to Him, and He talk to us just like He did with Adam.

Jesus' purchase not only enabled us to be physical friends with God the Holy Ghost, but also through Him, become physical friends with God the Father and Jesus Christ, to have two sided conversations and dialogue with them, experience their feelings and emotions and enjoy them as individual personalities through the Holy Ghost. Jesus' purchase allows me to approach so closely to Him that I could physically climb up onto His lap, give Him a big kiss on His cheek, and tell Him how much He means to me and that I love Him, and hug Him completely, without any reservations. One day I will do these things to my Father who is in Heaven and to Jesus my Brother who is the King of Heaven, but for now I am left with a close physical relationship with the Holy Ghost who lives on the Earth.

During those countless midnights we spent worshiping together at university, I would get the urge to walk over to where the Holy Ghost was standing, and just as a child would stand on His Father's feet when learning how to dance, I got the urge to stand on the exact spot where He was standing. When I placed my feet on His feet, my body and head automatically aligned to where His body and head were so that I was standing in Him and in His space. In this position I felt His power running up and down my body. He was cool, energizing and electrifying, yet He was laced with joy, so much joy it was uncontainable. What a feeling! It was the most intimate place to be because one actually got into the personal space of God the Holy Ghost. So whenever I needed more of Him or craved maximum intensity of His Presence, I would go over and stand in Him - in His Manifest Presence.

God has hugged me many times when we were alone, but the most memorable hug was the first time He did it in public. It was at the Living Room cell group when He came running in like a Mighty Rushing Wind, and He wrapped His wings around me. Being hugged or held by God is an unforgettable experience. David wrote in the Psalms (Psalms 63:7; 91:4; 17:8; and 57:1) how the Holy Ghost protected him by wrapping him in His wings. (These references show that the Holy Ghost has wings that He can wrap around us to comfort us while Luke 3:22 shows that the Holy Ghost can take the form of a dove.) David was talking about God the Holy Ghost here not the Father or the Son. Like a dove, He has wings; however, there are times He has hands and can touch you or tap you with His fingers—the same finger with which He wrote on the wall before Belshazzar (Daniel 5:5; Psalm 63:8; and Psalm 17:7). The Holy Ghost showed me this a couple of weeks after the cell group incident, explaining that in the worst of times the same wings with which He held me, He held King David of Israel and I felt very privileged. To this day, on those really terrible days when all hell breaks out against me and when the suffering goes on one week after another, I keep holding onto God's promises to me throughout it all, and I still go to Him for a hug. This gives me life and encouragement to keep holding onto Him and His promises. In these times, God hugs me especially when there is no one else around to console and hug me and give me any real comfort or peace.

By *peace,* I mean *peace* that transcends all human understanding. Humans cannot give peace like this only God can, so the only way to get it is from Him. His hug not only gives me a supernatural dose of peace when I need it, but sometimes His embrace energizes or infills me, empowering me to continue to fight the fight of faith. He administers whatever you need or ask for when He hugs you. Sometimes He comes with deliverance as He did with my nicotine addiction at the Living Room cell group mentioned in chapter twelve.

There were times when God's Presence would fill my dorm to overflowing if I just blew Him a kiss. It started to happen around a time when I asked the Father to set my heart on fire for the Holy Ghost and to teach me more about Him. This was around the same time when I was just beginning to keep our date at midnight every night. Within a day or two, the Father answered my request. He started a season where I thought I would die without the Holy Ghost's Manifest Presence in my life, and I would rush home to my dorm from study group meetings or the library to see my Friend and hang out with Him. I could not get enough of Him. It was as though I was in love with Him, and for the first time, I understood what David the Psalmist meant when he called the Holy Ghost *the Lover of his soul.*

One night I was so overwhelmed to see His physical form walking around in my room, much like He walked around in the fire with Shadrach, Meshach, and Abed-nego (Daniel 3:25) and I was so grateful that He was in my life, that I could not express my feelings in words and so I blew Him a kiss. Immediately the atmosphere in my room changed, and He stopped in His tracks and looked right at me. I did it again, and He moved closer to me. I told Him how much He meant to me and that I needed Him to live this Christian life, especially at university where students were becoming very lonely and were getting into destructive relationships just to avoid being alone. Fortunately, there was no chance of that happening to me because He was always around me—talking, singing, and appearing every midnight. I was sure that He would keep me from harm. My heart was overflowing with gratitude, and I told Him that I loved Him for caring for me so much. Immediately, the room began to be filled to overflowing with His Presence–with more and more of Him. There seemed to be an air of anticipation or expectation that He was going to do something. This built and built until it could not get any higher. Then all of a sudden, He ran at full speed straight for me and hugged me. His huge and awesome Presence that filled my room to overflowing now hugged me. It was too much power and too much of His Presence for me to handle, so much so that my knees buckled and I fell under His power. I laughed and laughed, and so did He. I had never heard God laugh before. *He has a really nice laugh,* I thought.

"I love you too George," He said. "I love you too."

FROM MY BEDROOM TO THE WORLD

THE HOLY GHOST is more real to me than anything or anyone on this earth, and I could never live without Him. I have implored the Father many times that the way I feel about Him would never change and that He would never leave me.

As I mentioned earlier, we had a date every night at midnight that was spent worshiping the Father and Jesus, hanging out together, talking, and having fun together. Once I had wooed His Presence into my life, this went on every night throughout my university years. There was a young Jamaican law student who had led me in the sinner's prayer in 1993—three years before my salvation experience. I met her while studying sciences at the Cave Hill Campus of the University of the West Indies in Barbados. As God would have it, I met her again in Barbados a year after my salvation, and shared with her that all of my friends at the University of Buckingham went to England and found girlfriends and wives, whereas I went to England and found the Holy Ghost.

To this she promptly asked, "Who did better?"

I responded just as promptly, "I did!"

• • •

THOSE PRECIOUS NIGHTS together ensured that I was never lonely at Bucks. At midnight, we would talk and joke around, and He would remind me of all the comical things that happened during the day. The Holy Ghost is the funniest person I know. He has a witty sense of humor. I did not realize it at the time, but I became very attached to Him, and after a while, I did not treat Him as a Ghost or as a Spirit, but as a man. After all, He was the Manifest Presence of God on earth, and it was only fitting that I should treat Him with the utmost courtesy and respect. On those precious occasions when He appeared during the daytime, I did silly things like opening car doors for Him and holding them open until He sat down in the vehicle. I even held open doors to buildings and to my room until He passed through them. This was how real He was to me. After a while, some of my Christian friends noticed what I was doing and laughed at me. One night during our midnight worship session, I excused myself from the Holy Ghost's company and opened my bedroom door to go to the bathroom down the hall. At the same time, some Christian friends happened to be walking up the hallway. As they paused next to my door to chat with me, they could feel His awesome Presence and glory emanating from within my room, and some of their bodies and bones began to vibrate.

With tears running down their cheeks, they looked at me quizzically and asked,

"What are you doing in there?"

I smiled and replied, "The Holy Ghost is visiting me." Needless to say from that moment onwards, they stopped laughing at me. I often wonder what would have happened to them that night if He had come out into the corridor and followed me to the washroom as He sometimes did.

After a few months of opening doors for the Holy Ghost, He showed me how easy it was for Him to walk through them and comforted me, saying that it would not bother Him if I did not open doors for Him in the future. We laughed at how people reacted to me holding doors open for what appeared to be no one, and I agreed to stop doing it lest I soon found myself locked away in a sanitarium in some remote part of England.

* * *

FOR A VERY long time, the scheduled appearances of the Holy Ghost were limited to our midnight dates for worship. Ever so often, He would show up during the daytime if He wanted me to lead someone in the Sinner's Prayer and into the Kingdom of Heaven or if He wanted to show me something, but these were unscheduled visitations. I was awoken by my alarm clock every morning, and the first thing I did was to read my Bible for about an hour. Afterwards, I would pray to the Father and to the Son and talk to the Holy Ghost who was not even there yet, but I did it anyway. Breakfast and a shower were next on the agenda. I did this every single morning for many months until lo and behold, one morning I felt this intense electric charge in the air in my room. I was sound asleep, but this electricity was in the air around me and all over my room. I could feel power in my body reacting to this external power. I awoke to see the Holy Ghost standing at the foot of my bed with His glory turned all the way up and joy filling my room. I was taken by surprise and did not know what to say to Him. Then a phrase from Benny Hinn's book fell into my mind and instinctively rolled off my tongue, "*Good Morning Holy Spirit!*" I said. This was met by thunderous laughter from both of us because He knew better than anyone else how long I had waited to greet Him with these words. With all of our meetings taking place at midnight, it was just never possible to wish Him good morning. The mornings that I spent inviting Him to come and be with me as I read my Bible and prayed had finally paid off. It had taken quite a few months, but it was worth it. I rolled down the covers and sat on the edge of my bed looking for my Bible. He in turn came over and sat next to me on my bed. We talked, read, and prayed. It was totally different from my routine mornings because He was leading me in prayer to the Father and to the Son as well as explaining the Scriptures to me. These things which I normally did in my own strength were now being led by the Holy Ghost.

That morning I could have thrown away my alarm clock. It was of no use to me anymore. Because from that day forward, the Holy Ghost woke me every single morning, and He has been doing so ever since. He is consistently and reliably punctual, and His persistence is unyielding. He always woke me up with ample time to read, to pray, and to eat breakfast before attending classes.

There were a few occasions that He tried to wake me, but I just rolled over and resumed sleep, ignoring Him. In response He resorted to gently tapping my shoulder at regular intervals until I woke up and got out of bed. I have known Him to do this for a maximum duration of almost two hours. Other methods He used to get me out of bed included, pulling down the covers when I pulled them up over my head, and turning the intensity of His glory up higher until I woke up. On one occasion He even passed His hand up from the bottom of the bed, tapping me from the inside of my rib cage until I awoke and climbed out of bed. (He resorted to the latter in desperation because had I overslept on that occasion I would have been late for a final exam. Needless to say, that despite being taken aback with the sensation of fingers tapping on the inside of my sternum, I was very grateful to Him for waking me.) In the many instances when He tapped my shoulder, I could feel the sensation of definite fingers just like a man's hand. Needless to say, the first time He did this it spooked me. However, none of the methods of waking me mentioned earlier could compare to the special occasions when He was very pleased with me, and He entered my room in the early morning whispering over and over, "George, I love you. George, I love you." He would call my name repeatedly over and over until I could hear the sweet sound of His voice deep in my sleep telling me how much He loves me. I would awaken to His Manifest Presence standing in a corner of my room or sitting on the edge of my bed. There is no lovelier way to be awoken to face each day. None.

For a long time, I had God all to myself every morning and every midnight, but I was still alone during the long interval between breakfast and midnight. I was beginning to miss my Friend during this time as well. In fact something inside of me was yearning to have Him with me during my lectures. At this stage, any absence from Him for any period of time was quickly becoming unbearable. Having His Manifest Presence every morning and every midnight was not enough anymore. I needed more, more of Him in my life, more time with Him during the day, and more frequent appearances in my life. I complained to the Father repeatedly for a few days.

Up to this time, the only place I entertained the Holy Ghost was in my room. However, the urgent need which I now found within myself–missing Him during odd hours of the day and wishing He was with me at these times–presented me with a new problem—the problem of having to bring Him out of my room and into the world. I could not stay in my room and entertain Him during the daytime because I had lectures to attend, cases to read in the library, and grocery shopping to do. So I asked the Father if the Holy Ghost could accompany me wherever I went [If ye then, being evil, know how to give good gifts unto your children: how much more shall your heavenly Father give the Holy Spirit to them that ask Him? (Luke 11:13).] to which He responded, "Ask Him to come".

All those months in my room, it never dawned on me that all I had to do was to ask the Father for the Holy Ghost to always be with me, and He would be, just like the Bible says. This marked the end of an era and the beginning of an adventure. Now with constant invitations made directly to the Holy Ghost, I would draw Him unto myself and enjoy Him wherever I went. I would take Him from my bedroom into the world.

From that day, it began. You must realize that I did not set out to be able to have Him with me all day, everyday. No. I did not even know it was possible. A few days later, I was simply in a shop in Buckingham town center around lunch time, and I began to miss Him so terribly that my heart pined for Him. I immediately asked the Father if He would send the Holy Ghost to me in the shop to be with me at that moment. Then I said, "Holy Ghost, I wish You were here with me now. I miss You and can't stop thinking about You. I need You. Please come and be with me." Within moments, I could feel His electrical Presence keeping a little distance away at first, but at least He was there. I encouraged Him to come closer and to be with me, which He did. What a good time we had! We shopped together and hung out together, and I went all through the town center with Him. It was market day, and I really enjoyed my time with Him. I could hardly wait to spend another occasion like this with Him because we had so much fun together.

About three days later, I was in a lecture and thoughts of Him just popped into my mind again. So I closed my eyes and invited Him to come. A few seconds later, the air was charged with electricity, and I reopened my eyes to find that He was standing right beside me, keeping my company. Within minutes some of the people around me began to cry and to sniffle. All that remained was for them to openly burst into tears.

A few days later as the Holy Ghost walked into my room to wake me up for my first lecture–as He was now in the habit of doing–I invited Him to come to class with me. He very willingly came along accompanying me from my dorm to the lecture hall where He sat next to me at the back of the hall. He even helped me to take accurate notes as His memory is much better than mine, and then we left together. However, He did not attend all of my classes that day.

It took many constant invitations given by me almost daily, before the Holy Ghost spent an entire day with me. The way it happened was the more I invited Him, the more He came around and for increasingly longer hours, until eventually it was normal for Him to spend the whole day and night with me. When this stage had been attained, an average day was spent like this: He got me out of bed in the morning, we spent time together chatting and praying (this was how my morning prayer time went—a conversation with Him); we read the Bible, ate breakfast, attended lectures together, and had lunch together, went to more classes together, studied in the library together, went to the gym together, went for long walks together, had supper and studied until midnight together; at which time, we worshiped together as we had been doing for the past two years. Everyday was now spent more or less like this.

I also took Him everywhere I went. We went to the mall together, to the supermarket, and even to the beach together. He accompanied me absolutely everywhere. Wherever I went, He went, and wherever He did not want to go, I did not go. Now I had Him all to myself all day and all night long. When I was in Barbados on summer or Christmas breaks, He would hop into my car (I was still making a conscious effort not to open the car door for Him), and we would just take off together for the day. Sometimes He just wanted to stay home with me to talk, to worship, or to enjoy my company.

• • •

I REMEMBER GOING shopping for a very badly–needed pair of jeans in Leeds city center while visiting my younger sister in 1997. I spent the entire two week holiday in my sister's apartment with the Holy Ghost who read to me and explained in great detail the Book of Revelation. It was a fascinating yet terrifying experience at the same time as He showed me things to come that will befall the saints and the earth in the end times. However, I was in desperate need of a new pair of jeans, and I had told Him this. Yet every time that I made an effort to leave the apartment to go in search of the jeans, He beckoned me to come and open my Bible at Revelation. This continued everyday and every night for two weeks, which was how long and detailed His explanation of Revelation was, and at the end of it—two days before the end of my stay there—He woke me up early in the morning and said that today was the day to get the jeans.

I ate breakfast and showered, and we headed out. When we arrived in Leeds city center, I just walked with Him side by side as He walked past one jeans outlet then another and another. I asked Him why we were not going into the stores, and He was silent. He continued past four more outlets, and He did not flinch. He walked very confidently as though He knew exactly where He was going. Deep in my heart, I had wanted a pair of black Levi 501s, but I kept this information to myself. I never shared it with Him. Whenever I had set out to buy jeans in the past, there was always the ordeal of them not fitting me properly. Either the crotch was too low or the legs were too wide making them fit like crocus rice bags, or the crotch was too high and the waist was too small. It always took me about three to four hours to find a good fitting pair of jeans, and for this reason, I only went through this ordeal when it was absolutely necessary. We continued to walk until we came to a clothing store on our left hand side. He went in, and I got the urge to follow Him. There were jeans everywhere—many different brands, designs and colors. I approached shelves of jeans, but He was nowhere near to me. He was standing by another series of shelves that carried blue and black jeans. I approached Him only to see that there was a pair of black jeans untidily thrown across the others, which was in contrast to those that were neatly folded and placed on the shelves. He said, "Try it on." I picked up the same pair that was strewn across the others. It felt soft and had that strong store fresh smell that only new jeans can have. I headed into the changing room, examining it as I went in. It was a pair of Levis, and they were 501s. I slid one leg in, then the other and held my breath filled with hope, as I pulled it up to my waist. To my surprise, it buttoned! I was so excited! Again I held my breath and tried the zipper. It went all the way up very easily. I was in shock! The crotch was perfect, the length was just right, and the legs fitted perfectly. They fitted as though they were cut and tailored just for me, and they were so comfortable that I did not want to take them off. Never before in my life had I ever tried on one pair of jeans and bought them. Usually, it took a minimum of about six or seven. I thanked the Holy Ghost profusely for what He had done. Our jeans hunting expedition took a total of fifteen minutes. *Incredible!* I thought. *He is absolutely incredible!* I asked Him how He knew which brand of jeans I had my heart set on. I had purposely not told Him.

He just smiled at me and without missing a beat asked me while I paid for the jeans, "Can we go back home now and finish Revelation?"

"Of course," I replied. There was nothing else important to do. Sure there were things to see and do in Leeds city center and lots of shops to go into, but I would rather go home and hang out with Him.

• • •

NOW, IT BECAME my reality that I walked hand in hand with a Ghost, the Holy Ghost, wherever I went everyday of my life. He came everywhere with me, and I went everywhere with Him. We were never apart not even for a second. I would be in the shower, and He would be sitting on the toilet outside chatting away and spending time with me. Even while I was on the toilet, He would be there talking about something or leading worship. My life had become a twenty–four hour slumber party, hanging out with my Best Friend everyday, all–day long and all–night long. He would sit on my bed as I slept and would wake me early in the morning to worship, pray and to read the Bible with Him.

Occasionally when we were in the mall or the supermarket and people came into contact with me or stopped to talk to me, I noticed tears welling up in their eyes and running down their cheeks. Their throats became dry, and they would choke up all because He would be standing right there next to me, facing the person to whom I was speaking. The first few times that I witnessed these effects, I did not know what was happening. I realized that there was only a faint hint of His Presence with me in the mall, which was nothing in comparison to His intense and powerful Presence to which I had grown accustomed every midnight in my dorm in Buckingham, or in my bedroom in Barbados. However after a few instances of men and women starting to cry for no apparent reason, and some of them visibly shaking or vibrating uncontrollably right in front of me, I realized that this is what human beings experience when they are in close proximity to His Manifest Presence.

By the time that I was studying for my Masters of Law, my daily lectures had become a comical experience, and Ramón and I played games with it, observing the phenomenon where the Holy Ghost would come into the lecture hall with me and sit beside me (I always tried to find two empty seats near to one another, one for Him and one for me), and the people around us would begin to sniffle and tears would begin to fall. Their legs would begin to shake or tremble uncontrollably. Girls would cry, and we could hear them sniffling and watch them dry their eyes for the entire duration of the lecture. This happened at every lecture that I now attended. Occasionally I would leave the lecture to go to the bathroom. As I walked down the center aisle of students, they would start sniffling, their legs would start shaking, and sometimes the odd person would start weeping openly. I played with this phenomenon everyday for the first four or five months that it started occurring, and then I started sitting away from everyone else, keeping my distance so that I would not affect them in any way.

The grand finale was during my Masters examination in Securities Law which was held in the Chandos Road Building. Once again I had the experience of the Holy Ghost standing beside me and dictating to me what to write in the exam, and reminding me of the names and citations of cases for the entire duration of the exam just as He had done in every exam in every semester since my salvation. As usual the people sitting around me could feel the effects of His Presence. An Asian girl in front of me sniffled and dried her eyes for the entire three hour period of the exam, while another Asian girl sitting to my right continuously dried the tears which fell onto the paper she was writing on for the entire duration of the exam. After an hour into the exam, her legs could be heard knocking incessantly against the legs of her desk—*Rat-a tat-tat!* It went on for two hours continuously until the exam was over. Under normal circumstances, people would be annoyed by such an irritating disturbance especially under the pressure of an exam, but there was a thick joy that saturated the atmosphere in the room, and so people just smiled at the sound of the slight knocking and continued to write. So there she was; with her legs knocking against the desk legs beyond her control, drying her tears off the page with a tissue in her left hand, while trying to write her exam on the same tear–sodden page with her right hand. It was almost comical, and I felt sorry for disturbing her.

I asked to be moved to another seat to avoid the disruption I was causing. However seating was assigned, and there were no extra seats anyway. With that I heard a muffled outburst and looked up to see the source. One young man about seven people ahead of me just about managed to stifle his bursting into tears and was persistently drying his eyes with a handkerchief. The students sitting around him snickered at his little outburst. Only now that I was looking up did I realize the large number of people who were being affected by God's Presence standing on my right hand side, and the large radius of people who were encompassed by His Presence in the room. The radius was about six to eight people ahead and behind me, and there were only five people abreast. More than eight people in the room had their bones vibrating, as the knocking of their legs against the desk legs could be heard faintly, and next to me were many people who were in tears, sniffling and drying their eyes. The room was saturated with peace and joy, and I just continued to write everything My Friend whispered to me, trying to remain oblivious to all that was going on around me. As I got closer to finishing the exam, there was a cool Wind that began to blow through the exam room, and there was more joy in the atmosphere than ever before. It grew gradually stronger and cooler as I got closer to finishing.

• • •

SO NOW I had His Presence with me all day and all night long, twenty-four hours a day, seven days a week. I was never apart from Him nor He from me. Never. Not for a moment. He was with me continuously all of the time—never leaving me, never forsaking me, just like Jesus said He would do. "I am with you always, even unto the end of the world" (Matthew 28:20). "I will never leave thee, nor forsake thee" (Hebrews 13:5). Jesus' promise had become a manifested reality in my daily life; His ever-abiding Presence was a supernatural and physical reality every waking moment of each day and night. Today I am eternally grateful to the Father and to Jesus, that just by asking and inviting the Holy Ghost, I have the Holy Ghost manifested as an ever–present companion everyday of my life, and that to this day—He still is.

BIBLIOGRAPHY

Hinn, Benny. *Good Morning Holy Spirit.* Nashville, Tennessee: Thomas Nelson Inc., 1990. *Pgs.* 33–34

Give Thanks with a Grateful Heart lyrics written by Henry Smith

CONTACT INFORMATION

Tel: (246) 421–8187

Email: georgejhag@yahoo.com

Address: #2 Apt 1, Warrens Heights
Warrens, St. Thomas
Barbados, BB 23026

listen|imagine|view|experience

AUDIO BOOK DOWNLOAD INCLUDED WITH THIS BOOK!

In your hands you hold a complete digital entertainment package. In addition to the paper version, you receive a free download of the audio version of this book. Simply use the code listed below when visiting our website. Once downloaded to your computer, you can listen to the book through your computer's speakers, burn it to an audio CD or save the file to your portable music device (such as Apple's popular iPod) and listen on the go!

How to get your free audio book digital download:

1. Visit www.tatepublishing.com and click on the e|LIVE logo on the home page.
2. Enter the following coupon code: f2ed-49f5-3971-e2b8-0797-fd27-c637-ece8
3. Download the audio book from your e|LIVE digital locker and begin enjoying your new digital entertainment package today!